The Skinny on Teaching

What You Don't Learn in Graduate School

The Skinny on Teaching

What You Don't Learn in Graduate School

J. M. Anderson
Illinois Valley Community College

Information Age Publishing, Inc.
Charlotte, North Carolina • www.infoagepub.com

Library of Congress Cataloging-in-Publication Data

The skinny on teaching : what you don't learn in graduate school / edited by J.M. Anderson.
    p. cm.
Includes bibliographical references.
ISBN 978-1-61735-602-5 (pbk.) -- ISBN 978-1-61735-603-2 (hardcover) -- ISBN 978-1-61735-604-9 (ebook)
1. College teaching. 2. Effective teaching. I. Anderson, J. M. (Jeff M.)
LB2331.S554 2011
378.1'25--dc23   2011031952

Copyright © 2011 IAP–Information Age Publishing, Inc.

All rights reserved. No part of this publication may be reproduced, stored in a retrieval system, or transmitted in any form or by any electronic or mechanical means, or by photocopying, microfilming, recording or otherwise without written permission from the publisher.

Printed in the United States of America

CONTENTS

Preface		vii
Chapter 1	The Art of Teaching	1
Chapter 2	Yes, But Will They Remember?	17
Chapter 3	Speak, That I May See Thee	33
Chapter 4	A Little More Conversation	45
Chapter 5	Why Great Books Still Matter	59
Chapter 6	Layers of Reading	73
Chapter 7	What's Wrong with Academic Writing	87
Chapter 8	How *We* Can Save Liberal Education	107
Notes		113
Suggested Readings		129
Acknowledgments		133
About the Author		135

PREFACE

*I never intended to supply a method, but only to remove
the evils of contemporary education.*

~ Rousseau, *Emile*

Several years ago I was a visiting assistant professor at a liberal arts college, and every week the dean of students gathered new faculty to discuss some of the latest scholarship of teaching and learning. Most of my colleagues grumbled about those sessions, not simply because they felt obligated as new faculty to make an impression on the dean, but because they felt that those sessions didn't convey much that was useful. They politely listened to the dean, and chimed in the discussions here and there, but invariably they left feeling unsatisfied and unfulfilled. When I asked why, a common response was that the methods and techniques presented by the dean tended to make teaching seem artificial, stilted, or stiff. He might explain the mechanics of a grading rubric, or how to use classroom clickers to arouse student participation, but my colleagues were hankering to know what they *really* needed to be successful in the classroom. What they wanted was the skinny on teaching. That's what this book aims to give you.

I write from the trenches on front line. I claim to be nothing more than a noncommissioned officer talking about his experience to new recruits. The military analogy is not inappropriate. I was a sergeant in the U.S. Army, where I first learned about and took an interest in teaching. My interest deepened as an undergraduate student when I came under the spell of two fascinating teachers whose ability to stimulate students seemed unparalleled. Later, as a graduate student, I was a teaching assistant for three years to a rare bird in the academic world: a professor who is both a world-class scholar and an excellent undergraduate teacher. Imitation is a powerful instructor, and I was lucky to have had him as both a mentor and an example. Since graduate school I have taught lower-level, upper-level, and graduate-level courses at a community college, at 2 four-year liberal arts colleges, at a state university, and at a for-profit university. My field of interest is European intellectual history, with an emphasis on political thought and the philosophy and history of education. I am currently dean of Humanities, Fine Arts, and Social Sciences at a community college. I have been thinking about undergraduate education and teaching for more than twenty years.

My experience at that liberal arts college reinforced my view that modern scholarship of teaching and learning can hinder the aims of liberal education. That's because it often disregards sound methods rooted in concrete reality and the world of things, and because it ignores the long tradition of pedagogy from Plato and Rousseau to William James and Jacques Barzun. It claims to produce better teachers, but it tends instead to mechanize methods and reduce teaching to a system rather than approach it as an art that must be cultivated through practice, experience, and extensive study. The result is undergraduate teachers who (at best) know specialized teaching techniques but who (all too often) remain disconnected from the tradition of their profession and possess little or no knowledge of the inner philosophy of their art. In consequence, it leaves many graduate students and new college professors who are serious about teaching (like my former colleagues) feeling unsatisfied and unfulfilled.[1] One also might wonder how much it has contributed to the current crisis in higher education. Despite a proliferation of books and articles on the scholarship of teaching and learning, and of centers for teaching excellence (or something like them) on American colleges and universities over the past 40 years, students are increasingly graduating unprepared for the great world.

Consider some of the data. In *What Matters in College?*, Alexander Astin points out that colleges and universities are not engendering analytical skills and critical reading in their students. In a study of 24,000 students in a representative sample from large institutions, only 38.8% felt that they had become "much stronger" in critical thinking, and only 32.5% felt that their analytical skills were "much stronger."[2] The 2006 study by the National Commission on the Future of Higher Education showed that most college graduates have not mastered reading, writing, and critical thinking skills appropriate to their level of education. Since 1992, for instance, literacy rates among them have actually declined. The percentage of those proficient in prose literacy dropped from 40% to 31%, while the number proficient in document literacy dropped from 37% to 25%. Only quantitative literacy remained the same at 31%. But even at 40%, 37%, and 31%, the numbers are abysmal.

In fact, the commission concluded that, despite "increased attention to student learning results by colleges and universities and accreditation agencies, parents and students have no solid evidence, comparable across institutions, of how much students learn in colleges or whether they learn more at one college than at another." Even worse, an "unacceptable" number of graduates enters "the workforce without the skills employers say they need."[3] The 2004 report issued by the National Commission on Writing estimates that "remedying deficiencies in writing costs American corporations as much as $3.1 billion annually."[4] And the 2009 study by the American Council of Trustees and Alumni concludes that, even "as our students need broad-based skills and knowledge to succeed in the global marketplace, our colleges and universities are failing to deliver. Topics like U.S. government or history, literature, mathematics, and economics have become mere options on far too many campuses. Not surprisingly, students are graduating with great gaps in their knowledge—and employers are noticing. If not remedied, this will have significant consequences for U.S. competitiveness and innovation."[5]

Similar findings are discussed in several recent books, most notably, Derek Bok's *Our Underachieving Colleges: A Candid Look at How Much Students Learn and Why They Should Be Learning More* (2006); Anthony T. Kronman's *Education's End: Why Our Colleges and Universities Have Given Up on the Meaning of Life* (2008); Charles Murray's *Real Education: Four Simple Truths for Bringing America's Schools Back To Reality* (2008); Mark Bauerlein's *The Dumbest Generation: How the Digital Age Stupefies Young Americans and Jeopardizes Our Future [Or, Don't Trust Anyone under 30]* (2008); Andrew Hacker and Claudia Dreifus's *Higher Education? How Colleges Are Wasting Our Money and Failing Our Kids—and What We Can Do About It* (2010); Mark Taylor's *Crisis on Campus: A Bold Plan for Reforming Our Colleges and Universities* (2010); and Richard Arum and Josipa Roksa's *Academically Adrift: Limited Learning on College Campuses* (2011).

At this point you might be asking, "With so many recent books on higher education, do we really need another?" Yes, I answer, because none of these books adequately addresses the real solution to the crisis in higher education: intensified pedagogy. None discusses the nitty-gritty aspects of teaching; none attempts a synoptic and concise explication of the principles of the art; none shows teachers how to apply those principles while fostering the aims of liberal education; and none challenges modern theories of pedagogy or questions the assumptions of current scholarship of teaching and learning. In short, the authors of those books fail to show that *what we teach* and *how we teach* are inseparable from the aims of undergraduate education.[6] This book does.

It shows graduate students and new college professors that there is a viable (and in my view, a more interesting) alternative to the books on teaching currently available or in print. This alternative is the classic texts on education and pedagogy. These books make us better teachers, I shall try to convince you, because they force us to return to the basic principles of our art. They help us not only to pose the fundamental questions about teaching and education that all teachers should be asking, but also to resist easy and preferred answers by showing us others worthy of consideration. We should read and study these texts, take from them what is valuable, and develop our own methods and styles of teaching. I hope that my message will likewise appeal to high school teachers and veteran college professors who are disenchanted and seek some way to break free from their malaise. If you feel the same, or are looking for a straightforward, useful, and appealing guide to college teaching, then this book is for you. It is intentionally short, little, "skinny," so that you can read through it quickly but also peruse the chapters and mull over the topics at your leisure. You might not always agree with me, but at least you'll be thinking about (or rethinking about) what you do.

Chapter 1 is a synopsis of the principles of our art as I have distilled from experience and reflection, from conversations with students and colleagues, and above all else, from a few great masters who knew a thing or two about teaching and learning. Chapter 2 discusses memory and learning, but it also illustrates how some modern scholarship of teaching and learning largely reiterates what has already been said on the subject in some of the classics texts. Chapters 3 through 7 show teachers how to treat the four most fundamental (but often-neglected) functions that we perform—lecturing, discussions, reading, and writing—as essential acts of liberal education themselves. The last chapter offers five realistic solutions on how we—as professors on the front line—can do our part to revitalize liberal education.

By liberal education I mean broad instruction in the liberal arts that aims to imbue students with appropriate habits of thought and mind, especially skepticism, intellectual discipline, and judgment. I write from the premise that undergraduate education *is* liberal education and that liberal education should be the primary (although not exclusive) goal of every college and university. Traditionally, liberal education has been associated with free men and intended for the ruling class. In modern times it countervails mass society, or mass culture, and the tendency toward overspecialization. It will never be universal or truly democratic because it prepares us for the highest pursuits. However, it can serve modern society and democracy by preparing us to live as thoughtful and virtuous human beings, and by liberating us from vulgarity, which for the ancient Greeks meant a lack of experience in beautiful things. It takes us beyond the present by inviting us to listen to and participate in the great conversations of the ages. It not only enlarges our perspectives, it strips us of our provincialism, our smugness, and our naïve self-sufficiency which keeps us from imaging that people in other places and times might live and think differently from ourselves. Some might say that my idea of liberal education smacks of snobbery or elitism, but I would disagree.

Like many students today, I was neither ready nor prepared for college. I grew up on the South side of Chicago in a working-class family. My mother, a single-parent, raised my three sisters and me. No one in my immediate or extended family (except for one cousin) went to college, let alone to graduate school. College wasn't even an option, and I probably wouldn't have considered it if my high school director hadn't asked me at the beginning of my senior year where I planned to apply. After the army, I attended a liberal arts college where those two professors I mentioned above revealed to me the transformative power of liberal education. Rather than dismiss me or write me off or let me slide by because I wasn't college material, they introduced me to great books and forced me to read other difficult and challenging texts; they took the time to teach me to write; and they showed me by their example how a mature, learned, and disciplined mind approaches various intellectual questions. Above all else, they imbued me with the appropriate habits of thought and mind that defines the liberally educated person. For education to deserve to be called *higher*, it must produce something that separates those who receive it from those who do not.

That something is free and cultured human beings who, as Wayne C. Booth put it, can think their own thoughts, experience beauty for themselves, and choose their own actions.[7] That something is graduates who have broken free from their self-imposed nonage and developed character and good habits of living. Rousseau was right when he said that "there can be no training of the intellect which is not also a training of the character"—a point William James reiterates in *Talks to Teachers*, as do so many others who have thought long and hard about education. What could be more beneficial and practical than to see through shams, to know a good person when you meet one, to learn to live life well? Thomas Jefferson once said that a public institution must be judged by its effects on the collective human character. By this standard the majority of colleges and universities in the United States are in a bad way.

Our moment calls, not so much for innovation, as for recovery. We are at least a generation removed from the day when the ideas in the classic texts on education and pedagogy were widely promulgated and commonly known. In writing this book, I have sometimes felt like the humanists of the Renaissance whose rediscovery of ancient works sparked a re-birth in, among other things, education. Like them, I believe it is important to share my discoveries from books little read or long forgotten. More importantly, I feel compelled to speak out on behalf of authors whose voices are almost never heard, and whose ideas are largely ignored, in the conversation about teaching and learning that is taking place today. They are my chief sources, and I openly and unequivocally acknowledge my indebtedness to them.

If I quote from them inordinately and use language that is close to theirs, it is to show the relevance of what they say; if anyone accuses me of saying little that is new, I can only respond with the hope that I might make ideas that are old and unknown new again for our time.

The story of higher education in America doesn't have to end in tragedy, but it's heading that way unless modern educators recognize that teaching is the most difficult task that professors, especially new professors, undertake. It requires sustained effort through constant attention, thought, and work. Once we imbibe this basic truth, and practice it, the quality of undergraduate education will improve drastically in American colleges and universities. What's needed, says Jacques Barzun, is an "open conspiracy of genuine Young Turks who will turn their books on analysis and criticism and reinvent—say—the idea of the university, and show what it can do." While I could only hope to promote such a conspiracy, my more modest aim is to provide readers with a synoptic but concise explanation of the principles of teaching and introduce them to some of the great masters who can reveal the timeless truths—and yes, even the magic—behind the art.

CHAPTER 1

THE ART OF TEACHING

We are discussing no trivial subject, but how to live one's life.

~ Plato, *The Republic*

One of my favorite movie scenes is from *Good Will Hunting*. If you've seen it, you'll know what I'm talking about. The movie starts by showing students at MIT who can't wait for their professor to give them their next mathematics problem. When it is finally posted, they scramble to copy it and then return to the library or their dorm rooms to work it out. It's challenging and competitive and designed to be virtually impossible for them to solve. And when they can't, they look forward to their next class in which the professor reveals the answer and shows them where they made their mistakes. There's no better illustration of what higher education is all about. A short while later, we are taken to Bunker Hill Community College, where Robin Williams—no longer Mr. Keating of *The Dead Poet's Society*, but Sean Maquire, instructor of psychology—is teaching a survey course in his subject. He's brilliant, we learn later—even more brilliant than MIT Professor Gerald Lambeau, played by Stellan Skarsgård—but you wouldn't know that by looking at his students. Some are sleeping, some are gazing out the window, almost of all them look disengaged and bored. There's no better illustration of what higher education is all about.

I especially like that scene because it reminds me of my first teaching job at a community college. The experience was bittersweet for me. It was

---

The Skinny on Teaching: What You Don't Learn in Graduate School, pp. 1–16
Copyright © 2011 by Information Age Publishing
All rights of reproduction in any form reserved.

bitter because the standard teaching load was 5/5; classes were large (capped at 35 students each, but more were allowed if the dean felt it was necessary); almost all of my students were unprepared for college-level work; and too many were there because they needed to remain on their parents' insurance or didn't know what to do with themselves after high school or bought into the myth that you must go to college to be successful. The experience was sweet because I was dealing mostly with first-generation students like myself; I taught many nontraditional students (some of the best I've ever taught); I had the kind of freedom as a teacher that I haven't had since; and above all else, I acquired invaluable on-the-job training. In the army, some of the best officers were those who had enlisted first. More and more I'm convinced that, if you want to become an excellent teacher in higher education, you should teach at a community college or some place like it. And that's not to disparage community colleges or their professors, who are some of the hardest workers in the profession.

But it raises a question. Under such conditions, why would anyone want to teach at the college level? Of course, many do because they think it's an easy job that will give them plenty of free time for leisure or their research. Even with a 5/5 teaching load you still get winter breaks, spring recesses, and summers off. I often hear people say it's because we're in a noble profession or that we are shaping the next generation and hold the future in our hands. But that's all bunk. The good teachers—the best teachers—teach because it's their passion, their calling. Like poets and writers and artists and scientists, they are willing to endure hardship and obscurity, and in most cases forgo better-paying jobs, because they love what they do. They need to be in a classroom and cannot imagine doing anything else. Above all, they are willing to think about teaching and work hard to improve it, constantly honing their skills and cultivating the principles of their art. These cannot be condensed into a formula, simply memorized and routinely applied. Nor is teaching a cognitive skill. It is a complex activity that requires commitment of emotions and will. As with any other form of expertise, perfection must be earned through the trials-and-errors experienced by each teacher. No one has ever taught good teachers—let alone the best teachers—*how to teach*. Let's be clear about that. If you aspire to be a great teacher, the only path is through consistent practice and hard thinking and work. You must be intrinsically motivated and willing to accept the activity itself as the reward of your achievement.

On the first day of any given class you are likely to find professors telling students that they must take responsibility for their education, that they must be engaged in class, that they must make an effort outside of it, that they must.... But how many of us keep our end of the bargain? How many of us try to understand our students, their longings, their hungers? It should work both ways. We must strive to fulfill our duties and live up to our philosophy of teaching in the classroom just as we must strive to fulfill our duties and live up to our philosophy of life in our daily lives. If our subjects have relevance and meaning for us, it's because we have made them relevant and meaningful over many years. But the first and most difficult task of teaching is to show that to people who, for the most part, probably don't feel the same. There are many ways to do this, but let me suggest three ways to start.

First, set a good example. If the army taught me anything about teaching it was the importance of being a role model for my students. I do not mean this in the sense that I expect them to follow my example and join the service—although as I get older I am becoming more and more convinced that most students should postpone college until after serving in the military or the Peace Corps or holding a regular job for a few years—but in the sense that it taught me what it means to be a leader. My mentor in graduate school once compared the teacher to the captain of a boat who is both guiding and rowing it. The analogy is good because, like a good teacher, a good captain knows where he is going, how to get there, and how to bring others along. The analogy falls short, however, because a good captain, as a good leader, shouldn't have to row; he gets others to do it, even when they don't want to. Of course, in the army (or even your classroom) you can order people to do things, but that won't inspire confidence or respect.

Effective teaching is effective leading, and effective leadership means setting a good example. As teachers we must think about the kind of model we wish to be for our students, even in matters ostensibly unrelated to our subject. Is our grammar unexceptional? Are our manners vulgar or boorish? Do we dress appropriately? Are we coming across as arrogant, smug, or condescending? Impressions matter, whether we think it or not, and example is always more efficacious than precept, as Samuel Johnson reminds us.[1] If the scholar of Shakespeare is boring and the professor of biology lacks common sense, students are likely to conclude that studying Shakespeare or biology makes one dull or inept. Unfortunately, popular culture often reinforces such images, making the stereotypes that much harder for us to shed. In a television show like *The Big Bang Theory*, the scientists are geeks—smart and funny, yes, but still geeks; in *Friends*, the only remotely intellectual character is Ross, a paleontologist with a PhD, whose intellectual qualities make him laughable—like the time he affected a British accent while teaching at NYU. My students typically preferred the snarky Chandler.

Another way to set a good example is to show your students that you care about what you teach. If you are unprepared or apathetic, students are likely to question why they should be there, let alone work hard in your class. College students think that "professors cheat," Timothy Clydesdale points out in *The First Year Out*, when they "make no effort to update their classes, give the same exams each year, and require the same assignments," encouraging students by their own example to take the "easy way out."[2] That was my dissertation advisor, a brilliant, world-class scholar but an awful undergraduate teacher. From the first year I met him he told me that he needed to change the one undergraduate course he had been teaching for about thirty years. And every year he changed nothing. That's because his other interests as an academic—chiefly his scholarship and his books—were more important to him than his teaching. We all have colleagues who do the same things and use the same material semester after semester, year after year. I knew one whose lecture notes were yellow and brittle with age. He complained that they were crumbling in class and he'd have to rewrite them. Although a veteran, and tenured, he didn't think about the example he was setting for his students. He just didn't care. I knew another who showed students a videotape of herself lecturing, sat down in the back of the classroom, and fell asleep. "What really makes a difference in education," Plato reminds us in the *Laws*, "—not only of the young but of ourselves—is not so much the precepts one gives others, as the way one exemplifies the precepts one would give to another, in one's conduct throughout life."[3]

Second, know your subject. Teaching is inseparable from learning and therefore inseparable from scholarship. Jacques Barzun defines the scholar–teacher as someone "who loves teaching, does it well, and continues to study his subject."[4] I would broaden this definition to include those who have not only mastered and researched in their specialty, but who continue to read as widely as possible in other subjects, particularly the primary sources, which should always be at the center of teaching. In this way, teachers also set an example by living up to the ideal of liberal education, or broad instruction in the liberal arts. They show that they possess expert knowledge in their subject and competence in their profession, and they demonstrate a wide range of knowledge through what they teach. In this way, too, they show by their example how to address issues and controversies of both yesterday and today, and how their own subject relates to the whole. After all, both our knowledge and example ultimately separate us from students and give us our authority to teach them.

Third, like what you teach. This might seem self-evident, but new professors are often asked to teach courses unrelated to their specialty or subjects of interest. Even veteran professors can lose enthusiasm for their topics by teaching the same courses year after year. Boredom must always be averted, even in teaching, which is another reason why teachers must stay engaged professionally and cultivate knowledge in a variety of subjects. I use literature, art, music, for instance, not only because they keep my teaching fresh and often shed new light on my subject, but also because they enable me to reach out and draw my students in with a variety of materials that they can relate to and understand. Subjects that resonate with students' lives will stimulate the appropriate response in them, as one of mine confirmed in an e-mail message when he wrote, "I have learned more about how the world works from past to present compared to any other class I have taken in my entire life."[5] When this happens, it is easier to help our students articulate their hungers while raising them to a higher level of awareness—which is the point of liberal education over mere technical or vocational training. Students need to feel that they are learning something worthwhile; teachers need to convey how their subject is meaningful to students.

Locke understood this, having observed in *Some Thoughts Concerning Education* that the best way to get and keep the attention of students is to show them that they can do something which they couldn't do before, something which gives them "some power and real advantage above others who are ignorant of it."[6] So did Rousseau, who wrote in *Emile*: "Relations of effects to causes whose connection we do not perceive, goods and ills of which we have no idea, needs we have never experienced—these are nothing to us. It is impossible by means of them to interest us in doing anything which relates to them." You are more likely to get the required reaction from students by selecting the areas that best illuminate your subject—and by often ignoring the minutiae of your dissertation or latest book or article. One of the best compliments I ever received as a teacher came from a student who acknowledged how many primary sources I must have read and how much drab material I must have scoured to find readings that appealed to him and the other students in class. I could have told them that my subject is useful and interesting, but that wouldn't have been enough; instead, I showed them that knowledge of my subject is useful and interesting, and stirred their passions. I learned from Plato and Rousseau that teaching is erotic and education an erotic pursuit.

Of course, one can teach and learn without eros, just as one can have sex without it, but one is not likely to be very good at either. The essence of teaching is explaining, which involves rhetoric; and rhetoric, according to Socrates in Plato's *Gorgias*, is the art of enchanting the soul. Socrates' own erotic charm as a teacher was described by his incurable pupil Alcibiades in the *Symposium*:

> When I listen to him, my heart pounds ... it's a sort of frenzy ... possessed ... and the tears stream out of me at what he says. And I can see a lot of other people that he's had just the same effect on. I've heard Pericles, I've heard plenty more good speakers, and I thought they did pretty well, but they never had an effect like this on me. My soul wasn't turned upside down by them and it didn't suffer from the feeling that I'm dirt. But that's the feeling I get from him and I know very well, at this moment, if I were prepared to lend him my ears, I couldn't hold out, he makes me admit that when there's so much I need, I don't look after myself.[7]

Socrates, himself a great teacher in Plato's dialogues, claimed to be an expert in erotics, the only subject he said he knew something about. As an expert he knows the different natures and types of souls of his students—just as the expert rhetorician knows the natures and types of audiences. Through erotic speeches he brings out the erotic desires in his pupils; he finds the right channel to the soul, taps into its energy, harnesses it, and guides it toward the beautiful itself. Modern science affirms the connection between eros and education that Plato and Rousseau told us about all along. The caudate nucleus in the center of the brain—which is responsible for general arousal, sensations of pleasure, and the motivation to acquire rewards—not only directs bodily movements and coordination, it directs the acts of paying attention and learning.[8]

Teaching and being taught are as much emotional as they are intellectual. Plato, Locke, and Rousseau knew this, too, and what they knew is affirmed by modern cognitive research.[9] David Sousa writes that emotion "is a powerful and misunderstood force in learning and memory" and that "emotions play an important role in human processing and creativity." How a person "feels" about "a learning situation determines the amount of attention devoted to it. Emotions interact with reason to support or inhibit learning." James Zull similarly informs us that our emotions are "very important and if we want to help people learn, *we must expect to encounter emotion, and we must take it seriously*. We cannot dismiss the learner's emotions, even when they seem trivial or unjustified to us." Therefore, the teacher's job is to "discover those bits and pieces" of information and knowledge that students have and to build on them because people learn by adding new experiences to their old ones.[10] Why? Because when learning something we "blend the old and the new, and in blending we create whole new networks. We construct our understanding using part of what we already know and part of what is new."

If teachers can stimulate the passions of students, they will stimulate desire and their interest to learn, as Cicero said of Socrates, who "used to observe that his object was obtained if anyone was by his exhortations sufficiently incited to desire to know and understand." Show students that a subject has personal value, make them feel like something important is at stake, and interest in it will increase. Reading the Bible or studying Plato's dialogues, dull to many, is useful and interesting to those who believe their salvation or acquiring wisdom depends on it. Students are passionate about all sorts of difficult and inherently meaningless things—snowboarding, sports, playing musical instruments, for instance—and learn them without compulsion precisely because they like doing these activities and feel that they get something out of them. Effective teachers will tap into that energy and try to get their students to approach their subjects with the same enthusiasm. But it is not enough to tell them about a subject's worthiness, you must get them to think and feel its worthiness.

It helps, as I've suggested, if instructors themselves are visibly moved by their subject, because young people especially tend to be drawn to things that are novel and appeal to their sensations, and because students are initially more likely to follow what their teachers do rather than what they say. The visual effect of a professor enraptured by her subject will make it more concrete and real, stir their desires, and gain their attention. Even technical subjects like physics or economics can be made more appealing to the young, writes William James in *Talks to Teachers*, if they are taught "with reference to the successive achievements of the geniuses to which these sciences owe their being."[11] Teach subjects historically and they will take on humanistic value. "Not taught thus," James continues, "literature remains grammar, art a catalogue, history a list of dates, and natural science a sheet of formulas and weights and measures." In short, if teachers demonstrate that their own passions are stirred, and can emphasize how a subject affects students directly or touches something close to them that they can relate to, then its value will increase significantly in their students' eyes.

Most of the great masters agree that education works best, and instruction is more personal, when it moves from the particular to the general, as people do with experience. I always introduce a new subject with a specific, short reading that students can grasp. In my survey course on Western Civilization, for instance, my first assigned reading (on the second day of class) is a selection from Leon Battista Alberti's treatise *On the Family*, written in the fifteenth century. Alberti was a humanist who discusses, among other things, the proper roles of men and women in marriage. I ask students to tell me what the selection is about, what they understand, what they think is commonplace or peculiar, and what they make of it by comparing what Alberti says with their own views.

What they don't immediately grasp, is that by identifying particular details from the reading—such as the expectation that the wife should be obedient to her husband, that her proper sphere is in the household, or that the man is significantly older than the woman—I am introducing them to generalities about Italian society, which they will corroborate with other readings as the course proceeds. More importantly, I am showing them from the outset how to think about primary sources historically. This approach is not limited to history or the humanities. A chapter from Edwin Abbot's *Flatland* could be used to introduce students to geometry, or a puzzle might be used to get students to think about the principles of logic. The idea is to establish a common foundation and reference point—or put somewhat differently, to give your students an experience—so that learning can properly take place.

But focusing on particulars is not the same thing as overwhelming students with excessive details of scholarship, a common tendency among new professors—who also commonly go to the other extreme and lose their students with generalizations and theories when they have not yet grasped the particular knowledge upon which those generalizations and theories are built. As Whitehead points out, the "true practice of education must start from the particular fact, concrete and definite for individual apprehension, and must gradually evolve towards the general. The devil to be avoided is the cramming of general statements which have no reference to individual personal experiences."[12]

I'm convinced that's why nontraditional students initially perform better in school than traditional students, even though I have no data to support it. It is precisely because they have experience in the world, and can more readily relate that experience to the subjects they study, that they are more interested in learning. My observation is corroborated by Earl Shorris's success with his students in the Clemente Course at Bard College, and by Rebecca Carter, professor of biology at the University of California at Berkeley, who volunteers as an instructor at San Quentin. "I've been teaching on the Cal campus and teaching at the prison at the same time, and they were significantly more engaged when I was in the prison," says Carter. "Not always more in command with the subject matter, but more engaged, doing the homework, asking questions because they were passionate about learning."[13] Students who lack such experience need first to be drawn in by material they can relate to and understand to increase their interest in the subject and their desire to learn. Only after the mind is led from the particular to the general, and then back from "general notions to actual knowledge of the particular things," is one said "to acquire knowledge," as we learn from St. Thomas Aquinas.[14]

Aquinas explains the two fundamental ways of acquiring knowledge. One way is by *discovery*, in which natural reason reaches knowledge of unknown things by itself; the other way is by *instruction*, when someone else aids the learner's natural reason. Instruction occurs when a teacher leads students to knowledge of things they do not know in the same way that the person who learns by discovery directs himself to acquire knowledge of something he does not know. In other words, instruction is aided discovery. The act of learning takes place when the signs that the teacher manifests to his students stimulate and reproduce in their minds the reasoning process which students would go through if they were learning by discovery or their own natural reason. Put somewhat differently, teaching is the act of establishing the patterns of thought and reasoning that exist in the teacher's mind in the minds of his students. The teacher is successful when his students make those patterns of thought and reasoning their own. When this happens, his students are *thinking their own thoughts*. They have achieved understanding. Through this "instrumentality," Aquinas adds, they have learned something because they possess knowledge of things they did not know. We might say that knowledge has been transferred from the mind of the teacher to the minds of his students. But if the teacher is not understood, if what has been transmitted remains cloudy in his students' minds, then his students have not truly learned. They do not possess knowledge but merely a fuzzy notion or an opinion or a belief at best. When "a man is said to cause knowledge in another through the activity of the learner's own natural reason," this is teaching.

Modern cognitive scientists reinforce Aquinas' explanation that people learn from particular experiences and work toward a general understanding of things.[15] Rather than seeing their job "as giving students new information, facts, or concepts," writes James Zull, teachers must be as concrete as possible, which means putting "more effort into finding the old" and giving students "incentives and support" in using what they already have in their brains. Students learn "by selecting the right neuronal networks from among those that already exist." This gives them new experiences and shows them new things, which leads to thinking their own thoughts. This is simply another way of explaining that the most effective kind of teaching is aided discovery, as Aquinas says.[16]

Only Zull calls it transformation. First, the act of learning means the ability to turn past thoughts into action. Second, it means transforming "the source of knowledge from outside ourselves to inside ourselves." Because experience takes place outside of us, the brain must turn it into knowledge and understanding. At this point, we "no longer need to repeat, or even remember, exactly what we experience from the outside." When this happens, this new knowledge and understanding comes from within; it is transformed, since we have taken "ownership of knowledge"—which is another way of saying that we are *thinking our own thoughts*. Third, the act of learning entails a transformation of power. Once we "bring our entire brain into learning, we will find control passing from others to ourselves. We will know what we need for further learning and we will take charge of getting it rather than remaining dependent on others."

I realize that it is easier to say, "start with particulars and work up toward more general notions," than it is to do, so let me give an example from my own experience—how I teach a subject as big as the Scientific Revolution in my survey of Western Civilization. Students read about and we discuss the achievements of Copernicus, Kepler, and Galileo, and together we go over broader trends and advances, such as the discoveries in mathematics, the invention of new instruments, the creation of scientific societies, and the achievements in chemistry, anatomy, and biology. But I emphasize—and spend most of my time on—the new method. First, because it is a particular instance that will allow me to develop and make the larger points about the Scientific Revolution; second, because of its pedagogical value.

Students read significant extracts from Francis Bacon's *Novum Organum* (1620) and Rene Descartes' *Discourse on Method* (1637), which we discuss, dissect, analyze, and outline. While doing this we *discover*, among other things, that both authors are addressing the same epistemological issue, or foundation of knowledge, which I get students to formulate as questions: What is the nature of knowledge, and How do we know what we claim to know? This discovery turns the readings into a concrete problem which they can solve. Both Bacon and Descartes point out the common difficulty that most people face when trying to acquire knowledge of a subject, making sense of all the information before them. Bacon's solution is Induction, through which understanding is not allowed "to leap, or fly from Particulars, to remote, or the most general kinds, of Axioms, at once," but rather, it must proceed step by step, "like real Stairs, uninterrupted or broken" from "Particulars to lesser Axioms; and so on to middle ones; from these again to higher; and lastly, to the most general of all."[17] His foundation of knowledge is empirical, since the "lowest Axioms differ not much from bare Experience" and lead us to the middle axioms, which are "real" and "solid;" these axioms then lead to the most general, which are "not metaphysical" or "notional, theoretical, and of no Solidity" but "justly limited by these intermediate ones."

Descartes' solution, on the other hand, is Deduction, or the process of reasoning in which a conclusion follows necessarily from the stated premises. Like Bacon, he seeks to establish a reliable foundation of knowledge, but unlike Bacon, his rests on rational premises, for which he offers four steps to ascertain their certainty: (1) never accept anything for true unless you can be absolutely certain that it is true because it presents itself clearly and distinctly in your mind; (2) break up every idea into as many parts as possible; (3) ascend "little by little" or "step by step" from the simple to the more complex; (4) review every case so completely to make sure that nothing was omitted. When students can explain these two methods they have correctly answered the questions and solved our "problem."

The pedagogical value of these readings comes from the genuine *synergy of learning* that takes place in the classroom. First, I am actually teaching my students through aided discovery, according to Aquinas' definition, because I have succeeded in getting them to think their own thoughts. I am not simply telling them what Bacon and Descartes say, which is what a textbook or a lecture would merely do; rather, by making them go through the authors' arguments and recreating them in their own minds, and by having them demonstrate to me through outlines, explanations, and papers that they understand their arguments, I am giving them *knowledge of* the methods of Induction and Deduction. Second, I am teaching students specific content about the Scientific Revolution, such as why Bacon and Descartes were attacking the Schoolmen of the Middle Ages, and why both demanded that knowledge be "useful" and "practical," thus making them "modern" figures. Third, I am teaching them skills, such as reading and writing—I'll discuss how in later chapters. Fourth, I am imbuing them with the habits of thought and mind essential for a liberally educated person, based on my definition above. They develop skepticism, and learn the value of doubting, not only through the examples of Bacon and Descartes (which is partly why I have chosen these selections from these particular authors), but also through their own their own critical reading of these documents; they develop discipline through analyzing and outlining and explaining the arguments; and they cultivate judgment through selection and comparing and contrasting these authors and their works.

All these efforts are undertaken simultaneously to promote the greater aims of liberal education. Attentive readers may also have noticed that they place great emphasis on teachers *to show as they teach, and to teach as they show*, which is what I have just done. My use of Bacon and Descartes in teaching the Scientific Revolution gives students a concrete experience with the subject, but it also reinforces what Aquinas and other great masters teach us about learning that education works best when it moves from the particular to the general and from the general back to the particular. When John Cheke, the great sixteenth-century educational theorist and tutor to Edward VI, was asked why Xenophon's *Cyropaedaia* was just as important as Aristotle's *Ethics* to the prince's education, he answered that although the mind must be grounded "in those universal and timeless precepts and categories of virtues and vices," it was the "everyday examples of conduct which are amply displayed in histories" that "bring sound judgment to the particular." Young minds are rarely "sharp enough to penetrate into abstruse and recondite thoughts that are thoroughly necessary for corroborating any judgment about specific issues." Therefore, good teachers never "advance any precept without illustrating it with a noble example."[18] Nor do they let others select the material for their own courses for them. By deferring to the publishers of textbooks, the editors of readers, the scholars of teaching and learning, it becomes more difficult to create genuine *synergy of learning* in the classroom and foster the aims of liberal education.

Of course, none of this will occur if teachers don't like their students or enjoy interacting with young people in groups. It is, I admit, a difficult task trying to understand the natures of the young, and as teachers we are at a disadvantage. We are working against the forces of their upbringing, family life, and time. We may spend about three hours a week with them, during which we must compete with their other courses, their extracurricular activities, and their preference for entertainment and social life. Another difficulty is attuning oneself to the needs of different minds and levels while providing a common denominator. Rousseau's tutor in *Emile* had an advantage because he taught only one student. That's not possible, or even preferred, in higher education, but the trick is to make each student feel as if his or her interests alone matter.

I use the Socratic method during discussions, and even lectures, because it forces my students to get involved and it forces me to connect with my students. I hold tutorials in my office, not only because most of my students need remedial work, but because I remember from my own undergraduate experience how important the personal attention I was getting from my professors was to me as I struggled to write. The point is to get my students to see me as a human being who takes an interest in their lives both inside and outside the classroom. It would be easier to treat them as like types, but that would also be the lazy approach, as Pascal reminds us. "The more intelligent one is, the more men of originality one finds. Ordinary people find no difference between men." It is essential therefore to treat students as individuals, which they are striving to become, and to cater to their differences.

Another advantage of getting to know students is that it becomes easier to discover what topics interest them so that they can be related to their native interests. To return to my survey course on Western Civilization for a moment, I use Boccaccio's *Decameron* because it consists of many stories that are racy and controversial and deal with religion and sex. (These always appeal to the young, as do examples from music, television, and current movies.) Boccaccio himself says that he intends to entertain and instruct his readers, and he does, but his book gives students additional insights into attitudes toward women during the Italian Renaissance, which they can relate to the Alberti piece mentioned above. My selection makes it easier to stimulate their interest by connecting the first objects and experiences with later objects and ideas, step by step, working from the particular to the general and back again. Furthermore, by tapping into the native interests and energy of the young, rather than armoring myself against them, I can channel and use them to my advantage. Most graduate students and new college professors are still relatively young and can benefit from their age, but even older teachers who are supple and youthful in the classroom will be more attractive than young teachers who act like geezers.

That was the bookish tutor Oscar Maironi in Owen Wister's short story, "Philosophy 4." Oscar was studious, serious, and possessed a "great power of acquiring facts." His notebook alone was some 300 pages of lecture notes taken almost verbatim. (A professor once asked to see it to remind him of something he had said.) He disdained the "criticisms, slangy, and abrupt" way of the students he tutored, which "struck the scholastic Oscar as flippancies," but he felt compelled to indulge them because they paid him. Although "alive for 20 years," he "never yet had become young." His "love was not for the education he was getting" but for showing off. He was a prig and the perfect pedant—the best sign that liberal education has failed.

In short, Oscar was smug. He believed he had gems in his head that other students should recognize as valuable and desire as he did. All too often academics act like lovers and make the same erroneous assumption as those under Eros's magic spell: simply because they love their subject they think that everyone else ought to love it too. This is a big mistake among new teachers—and the biggest source of frustration. "Why can't students see how valuable this is," they are likely to ask. "Why don't they care?" We should meet them halfway, rather than assume, like Oscar, that our students' ambitions are like our own. The simple fact is that most of them will not become academics, or do not even wish to become academics; the sooner we stop teaching them as if they were all planning to attend graduate school in our subject, the better.

Oscar was also bitter. He resented his spoiled peers because he "had given his education to himself; he had for its sake toiled, traded, outwitted and saved. He had sent himself to college, where most of the hours not given to education and more education, went to toiling and more toiling, that he might pay his meager way through the college world." I have known teachers who resented students who drove more expensive cars than they did or whose parents gave them more spending money each month than they had disposable income. They remembered how they struggled and worked and sacrificed to go to school—and are now repaying hefty student loans—while these students squandered opportunities they only dreamt of having at their age. Resentment made them poorer teachers, less capable of bridging youth and maturity for their students.

Professors who are themselves liberally educated, and who practice the virtues of liberal education, will be better able to understand the natural development of the human heart and the general bent of their students. Their minds will be lively and they will be capable of relating what they teach to the broader world. Having wit and urbanity, they will never be at a loss to show students that what they are teaching is as much about life as anything else they see in movies or on television, even more so. Having real-world experience, they will show students how they have incorporated what they teach into their lives. Many students have told me that my passion makes me more attractive and effective as a teacher. They admire my nonacademic (including my military) experience and that my interests (as a certified personal trainer and a tutor for adult literacy, for instance) are not confined to the classroom or the archives. Most undergraduate students are hungering for good examples and meaningful instruction because the fast food they are fed in high school leaves them unsatisfied. When we don't give it to them, naturally they look elsewhere. We can blame students when our subject fails to intrigue them, but we should first look at ourselves, and think about how we can make our subject more appetizing.

I'm not saying that we must pander to our students or pretend to be something we are not, which will backfire when they see through the sham. I am saying that *we must learn about our students from our students* and establish our impressions with care because they affect the classroom environment throughout the semester or term. Students will be turned off if professors are inflexible or domineering, if they are pedantic or wear their learning heavily. They appreciate magnanimity, kindness, patience, even humility. Leo Strauss always advised his graduate students about to embark on their teaching careers to look out for the "one silent student in your class who is by far superior to you in head and in heart." Humility and patience must be observed because students are not equally intelligent or motivated to learn. It's easy to get frustrated with them for not paying attention, reading, participating in class, or doing the work; it's also easy to assert one's authority, bully them, or to lash out with irony or sarcasm—which is really an attempt to reinforce intellectual superiority and reassert one's power. This is a mistake. One sarcastic remark can wipe away the good impression and good will that you have been trying to establish, as I learned the hard way. Magnanimity, kindness, patience, and humility are virtues in anybody, but especially in teachers. So too is a sense of humor, Mark Van Doren reminds us. "Nothing in man is more serious than his sense of humor; it is the sign that he wants all the truth."[19] A good laugh at the right time can sometimes make the point better than the most brilliant lecture. Retain your eccentricities and quirks—which in many cases will make you more endearing to your students—but earn their respect. Before being Master of This or Doctor of That, be a human being first.

Here's my response to Oscar and professors like him: If our knowledge is valuable and worth having, it is up to us *first* to make it accessible to our students, and *then* to raise them to a higher level of awareness. But most professors today do the opposite and "lament how little the public takes notice of their scholarship or areas of expertise," writes Timothy Clydesdale. They might change this "by learning how to honestly communicate with that portion of the public seated directly in front of them: their students." Students are listless because they are bored; most think their general education classes are useless and that undergraduate education is irrelevant to their lives. Professors reinforce these perceptions, adds Clydesdale, by typically subscribing to "a set of educational goals that are wholly out of step with student interests."[20]

And no wonder, if they experience in their classes what one student describes in an open letter to professors: "If you literally read off of a paper for an hour and fifteen minutes, this does not count as a lecture. Everyone will either be asleep or hate you. I had a professor once do this for the full 14 weeks of the semester. She would often pause and look up at us, as if expecting some sort of a reaction. What did she expect us to do? Stand up and break out in raucous applause?"[21] No wonder, if they think about their classes what one of my students thought about Western Civ. II, which she was required to take: "This class sux," she wrote in an e-mail. She had taken Western Civ. I with me, also required, and told me how she preferred my methods and style of teaching to her current professor's because he was hypercritical and seemed to care only about cutting things down. Her comments resonated with those of a student in another class who once compared the bourgeoisie in Flaubert's *Madame Bovary* to many of his teachers. There might be something to his observation. How many provide students with inspiring and permanent models, or convey that wholeness is the end of education and the real good? Like Emma Bovary, students are longing for something better or higher; when professors don't give it to them, they look elsewhere for fulfillment. Or they simply shut us off.

The way to make undergraduate education meaningful is to make students feel as if what they are studying *has intrinsic value*. In other words, it is up to teachers to make their subject interesting—and "to say that an object is interesting," writes William James, "is only another way of saying that it excites attention." The best way to help students learn, reiterates modern cognitive scientist James Zull, "is to find out what they want, and what they care about," because learning "is a natural process when it has to do directly with the life of the learner." People will learn if they believe what they are learning is important to their lives. Therefore, teachers must *help them see how what they are teaching matters to their lives*.[22]

Teaching requires the ability to explain to others what is vague and unknown. If necessary, it also requires showing students every step and helping them to put these steps together to perform a task or demonstrate their understanding. Effective teaching requires teachers who are sensitive to the difficulties students face, who do not assume that they know beforehand how to perform the task or understand the material, and who create their own courses and think about what content to include; they must be patient and tolerant because the subject is new to students, who will fumble; they must be humble and remember that their subject is easy to them because they have been doing it for years. All teachers—but especially veterans—should take up some hobby or learn some new subject wholly unrelated to their field to remind themselves of the difficulties of learning something new. Perhaps the best thing I ever did when I started teaching was to take up Judo.

Finally, and above all else, graduate students and new college professors must remember that teaching is not simply a system of methods, but an art whose principles must be cultivated and practiced to be mastered, as Descartes reminds us in the *Discourse on Method*: "something cannot be conceived and made one's own when it is learned from someone else as well as when one discovers it oneself." Reflect on what you do. After every class think about why certain things worked and why other things failed. In the army, after every operation, we conducted an "After Action Report," through which we (1) identified problems, unforeseen issues, and what needed improvement; (2) came up with ways to fix them; and (3) were clear about the lessons learned.

Ineffective teaching has less to do with the traditional methods than it has to do with teachers who don't know the fundamental principles of the art, who don't pay attention to what they do and try to improve it, or who don't take the time to learn the natures of their students. That's why vogue phrases like "active learning" and "student-centered learning" are not only silly but meaningless. Learning is always active and about the student, otherwise, it won't take place.[23] The principles of teaching must serve the function of learning by stimulating a response or reaction in students that would otherwise take place naturally. It means getting them interested enough in one's subject so that they will remember what they are taught. It means developing the habits of thought mind through repetition and discipline. It means overcoming the natural human tendencies against work, authority, and concentration. Effective teachers have the will power to resist these tendencies, they have confidence in themselves, and they have the skills and the ability to practice their art. Perhaps most important, they know when to stop.

CHAPTER 2

YES, BUT WILL THEY REMEMBER?

To have understood without retaining does not make knowledge.

~ Dante, *Divine Comedy*

People are naturally curious and like to learn. It's why Jane Austen is still read and why the BBC production of *Pride and Prejudice* was a big hit; why such books as Doris Kearns Goodwin's *Team of Rivals* and David McCullough's *John Adams* were bestsellers; why exhibits like King Tut and Body Worlds are popular and sell out at museums across the country; and why so many high school and college students like the History Channel and the Discovery Channel. So why is it that as soon as we bring literature, history, or science into the classroom students have a tendency to turn us off?

One reason may be that most people are incapable of serious or demanding academic work. Charles Murray estimates that only 10–20% of undergraduates posses the intelligence or the ability (or both) to do college-level work.[1] If on top of that the other 80% lack good study habits and the skills to reinforce ideas on their own, it only follows that they will fail to retain information and learn what they are supposed to learn. Another reason may be that most people lack mental discipline. The "brain is not very good at thinking," writes cognitive scientist Daniel T. Willingham. In fact, it is not designed to think. Thinking is "slow and unreliable," and the brain has evolved "to save us from having to think."[2] If students naturally resist thinking, and most lack will or self-motivation to learn a subject, it also follows that they will get bored or reluctantly do what's required. The result is inattentiveness and poor performances in school.

Now I agree that there are many students in college who shouldn't be there, and that the human body (including the mind) is an amazingly efficient machine. As a teacher, I can attest to the former, and as a certified personal trainer, I can affirm the latter. For instance, I know that athletes will stop seeing gains in performance, and even ordinary people will fail to shed those last five pounds, if they follow the same exercise routine for weeks or months on end. Like the brain, the body adapts itself to the workload, and the more accustomed it becomes to exerting itself, the more efficiently it performs. This is a good thing from an evolutionary standpoint, but not so good for improving performance. As a trainer, my job is to prevent this from happening by finding new and different ways to challenge my clients and force their bodies out of complacency, so to speak. As teachers, our job in the classroom is pretty much the same. Students are more likely to learn, and to remember what they have learned, when we find new and different ways to challenge them and force their minds out of complacency. The essence of effective teaching is to stimulate a response or reaction in students that would otherwise take place naturally.

In *Talks to Teachers*, William James explains why. Education is little more than a "mass of possibilities of reactions," and every "acquired reaction is, as a rule, either a complication grafted on a native reaction, or a substitute for a native reaction, which the same object originally tended to provoke." Indeed, for James, the art of teaching "consists in bringing about the substitution or complication, and success in the art presupposes a sympathetic acquaintance with the reactive tendencies natively there." Therefore, the first and most important function for teachers is to get and hold their students' attention. The way to do this is to associate "the new with the old in some natural and telling way, so that the interest, being shed along from point to point, finally suffuses the entire system of objects of thought."

The problem is that attention comes in beats, lasts only momentarily, and cannot be sustained continuously. The act of attending to something exhausts itself in a single moment; therefore, maintaining attention requires the subject to reveal itself in new aspects or ways. It must prompt new questions, for instance, emphasize the subject from a new angle, or show how it is related to another subject. Put more simply, the subject must change. If it doesn't, attention wanders away, as Locke also explains in his *Essay Concerning Human Understanding*. Ideas in our minds "do constantly change, and shift in a continual Succession," and it is impossible for anyone "to think long of any one thing" or "*have one self-same single* Idea *a long time alone in his Mind, without any variation at all.*"[3] When we teach, we are, in effect, creating a sense of motion through bodily movement and speech, what Aquinas calls signs. Understanding this is crucial for establishing attention and stirring interest because it is impossible for the mind to stay fixed on a single unmoving idea for an extended period of time. Teachers who dwell on the same point or are redundant generate tedium; when students are bored their minds wander.

Repetition is necessary for fixing the impression, but the movement of ideas in succession is essential for keeping attention, as Locke further explains. Because there is a "constant succession and flux of ideas in our minds," it is necessary for understanding to control the mind (gain power over it, Locke says) so that we are able "to direct that train of ideas" perpetually coming "into our thoughts by a constant succession." In this way, we can stay focused on the ideas that "are pertinent to our present inquiry" and "most useful to the discovery we are upon," and reject those that carry us away from our present pursuit. "I have discovered no other way to keep our thoughts so close to their business," Locke adds, "but the endeavoring as much as we can, and by frequent attention and application getting the habit of attention and application." If a student's attention strays, he suggests gently guiding his or her mind back to the subject at hand through an anecdote or a story or some related incident. An occasional swear word helps too.

But attention is not enough. Effective teaching requires getting students to understand the material, and to remember it, because as Dante reminds us, to understand without remembering does not make for knowledge. Despite current wisdom, students must retain facts and store their memories with certain things, even in some cases by rote. "Any piece of knowledge I acquire today," writes Emerson, "a fact that falls under my eyes, a book I read, a piece of news I hear, has a value at this moment exactly proportioned to my skill to deal with it. Tomorrow, when I know more, I recall that piece of knowledge and use it better." Mark Van Doren calls memory "the mother of imagination, reason, and skill." A short memory is the reason for shallow thought, he adds, and the reason for shallow thought a short memory.[4]

Once more William James explains why. Memory needs some type of cue or trigger to produce the required result. The cue is something "contiguously associated" with—that is, connected or related to—the thing recalled. When we think, we make associations between ideas which are not interrupted by other external sensations; thinking continues, and the mind remains attentive, so long as these associations of ideas flow uninterrupted. For ideas to stick, they must be associated with something that is already there. The mind disciplined to train its thought on these ideas is more likely to remember them. The reason is that memory depends on what James calls an "organized system of associations." Quite simply, the "secret of a good memory is the secret of forming diverse and multiple associations with every fact we care to retain." In other words, people generally have good memories, not necessarily because they are smarter than those who don't, but because they think about things (facts, ideas, data, experiences) as much as possible and in a variety of contexts and connections. They weave them into "the most systematic relations with each other;" the mind discerns these relations as it relates and compares these things and determines their value or relevance.

Unfortunately, James adds, there "can be no improvement of the general or elementary faculty of memory; there can only be improvement of our memory for special systems of associated things," which is "due to the way in which the things in question are woven into associations with each other in the mind." If teachers therefore want students to remember what they teach them, they must somehow enforce in students the habits of continuously applying their minds to the subject at hand. They must develop, in other words, their own associations by organizing one thing with another. Effective teachers work to build up "useful systems of association" in the students' minds that are concrete, real, vivid, and active. Associations are rooted in habit, and habit in feelings, which is why feelings often trigger the appropriate cues in the mind, and why learning is as much emotional as intellectual, as discussed above. It is these laws of association that run the mind, generate interest, and keep attention.

What Locke, Emerson, and James teach us about memory and learning is largely affirmed by modern cognitive science and reiterated by modern scholars of teaching and learning.[5] According to present thinking, there are two kinds of learning that the mind undertakes.[6] One is implicit, which "accumulates through repetition over many trials" and involves "association of sequential stimuli and permits storage of information about predictive relations between events." For instance, a person who has learned something implicitly may show improvements in performance of tasks, even though he or she may not be able to describe what has been learned. It is independent of the knowledge database within the individual's mind. The other type of learning is explicit, which also "often involves association of simultaneous stimuli and permits storage of information about a single even that happens in a particular time and place." It is conducive to memory because it creates "a sense of familiarity about previous events."

Explicit learning depends more on memory, of which there are basically two types: working and long-term.[7] Working memory is akin to consciousness and fundamental to humans for language comprehension, learning, and reasoning; long-term memory acts as a storehouse and allows people to retrieve information. Just as William James pointed out, it is developed by the association of facts and figures and other data, and the individual's ability to retain them. It is useful, and will affect behavior, only if it can be accessed. Access is triggered by the appropriate cue. The whole process of combining information, whether from one's environment or long-term memory, says Daniel Willingham, is what we call thinking. And the key to essential thinking is "knowing *how* to combine and rearrange ideas in working memory."[8]

Most modern cognitive scientists and psychologists also agree that working memory is another name for consciousness—which William James said involves both attention and short-term memory—and that consciousness is at the core of thinking and reasoning.[9] They also tell us—again like Locke and James—that consciousness is always changing. These "rapidly formed coalitions occur at different levels and interact to form even broader coalitions. They are transient, lasting usually for only a fraction of a second." Compared to, say, modern computers, the brain's neuronal coalitions act very slowly, but the brain "compensates for this relative slowness partly by using very many neurons, simultaneously and in parallel, and partly by arranging the system in a roughly hierarchical manner." This is why (I think) Willingham says that the brain is designed to save us from having to think, as noted above.

Now combine these factors. Learning depends on memory, or "the process by which we bring back to mind some earlier conscious experience."[10] Learning is active, as we like to say, because it and the act of remembering are both "conscious events." Once again, as noted previously, this is why emotions are such an important part of learning, and why instruction works best when it goes from the particular to the general. Both give students an experience that has been stored in declarative memory which can then be triggered by the right cue. When the cue triggers emotional memory, for example, we are not accessing the emotion itself (which is its own new experience), but rather the memory of "the consequences" of the emotion, or "the way we behave or how our bodies feel."

No doubt recent studies in cognitive science have expanded our understanding of the biological, chemical, and neurological workings of the brain in ways that Locke and James could never have imagined—and I am far from suggesting that we should ignore the latest research (as a primer, I recommend Steven Pinker's *How the Mind Works*). The science is impressive, even daunting to a nonexpert like me. But the question I keep asking is: Does it make us better teachers? Will knowing *that* the caudate nucleus directs the acts of paying attention and learning and *that* emotion and learning are connected explain how to trigger appropriate emotions in students to promote learning? Does knowing *that* the thalamus is an important anatomical structure for understanding consciousness have any bearing on the fact that consciousness exists or explain what consciousness means? Will knowing *that* memory is a "system property that also depends on specific neuroanatomical connections" make us more effective in the classroom? In short, does knowledge of the cognitive process produce judgment, wisdom, or translate into effective application?

Not necessarily, according to James Zull, himself a cognitive scientist and scholar of teaching and learning, who points out that knowledge about the brain and how it functions is distinct from what cognitive scientists tell us about teaching. As "science gave us more information," he writes in *The Art of the Changing Brain*, "teachers began to realize that this did not automatically produce better education. Neuroscientists could not tell us how to teach. In fact, biologists still pay little attention to our concerns. They are excited about science, not about education." That's why he and other cognitive scientists, such as Daniel Willingham, have attempted to bridge the gap.

For example, in *Why Don't Students Like School?*, Willingham tells us that successful thinking depends on four factors: information from environment; facts in long-term memory; procedures in long-term memory; and the amount of space in working memory. "If any one of these factors is inadequate," he adds, "thinking will likely fail." Therefore, teachers should give students "cognitive work that poses moderate challenge" and "problems" to solve. They must respect students' cognitive limits and clarify problems to be solved, since "curiosity is provoked when we perceive a problem that we believe we can solve." And they must know when to puzzle students (but in the right way), accept and act on variation in student preparation, and change the pace of instruction because students will lose attention if they feel confused. "Change grabs attention," writes Willingham. "When you change topics, start a new activity, or in some other way show that you are shifting gears, virtually every student's attention will come back to you, and you will have a new chance to engage them." Finally, he adds, learning takes place only when students remember what they have learned, which requires some form of repetition and drilling.

This may be true, and Willingham knows more about the brain than most people, but as teachers we still need to figure out for ourselves when to change topics, when to start a new activity, and when to shift gears. That takes judgment and wisdom, which come from hard work and repeated trials, from consistent study, attention, and practice, and from dedication to the act of teaching. It takes understanding not simply why our students think and do things in a certain way, but how we can arouse their interests, keep them attentive, and get them to think and do things in a way that promotes learning. It also takes knowing the natures of our students so that we can find the right kinds of assignments, create the appropriate classroom environment, and present the material in such a way that we stimulate a response or reaction that would otherwise take place naturally. Above all, it means finding the right combinations and applying them to foster the habits of thought and mind appropriate to the liberally educated person, what I have been calling a genuine *synergy of learning*.

Unfortunately, the ability to do all these things is an art and cannot be taught. Skills can be taught, principles explained, concepts illustrated, and suggestions can be made; but how well one performs them, and whether one succeeds, depends upon many variables, mostly intangible. It's like playing an instrument or a sport. Knowing how to read music won't produce harmony any more than being able to hit, throw, and catch a ball, even with proficiency, makes a professional athlete. As a personal trainer, for instance, I know that people who do the same routine week after week, month after month, will not achieve their desired results because their bodies adapt (it's called "muscle memory" for a reason). The physiological principle is the same for everyone, but what I do for a man in his fifties trying to lose weight will be different from what I do for a woman in her twenties training for a triathlon.

True, I apply my knowledge of anatomy and physiology; but my skills and techniques have been developed both through my own training and through practice, experience, and attending to what does and does not work in particular situations. I am effective as a trainer because I know the appropriate exercises for each client and how to combine them in such a way that I achieve his or her desired result. But knowing how to do something is not the same thing as actually doing it. Nor does it mean that you'll be good at it—otherwise, all cognitive scientists, neurobiologists, and psychologists would be good teachers simply because they know how the mind works. Teachers who ignore this are like anthropologists who study the brain and love. Helen Fisher, author of *Why We Love*, might be able to describe the chemical reactions that take place in our brains and the physiological changes that occur in our bodies when we fall in love, but she cannot explain what triggers those responses in individuals, or how we become good lovers. I'm suggesting here that, in addition to introducing us to the fundamentals of the cognitive process as it relates to teaching and learning, great thinkers and teachers like Plato, Locke and James can.

That's because these and other great masters point us in the direction of the history and philosophy of education in a way that most cognitive scientists and modern scholars of teaching and learning do not. They get us to pose the fundamental questions about teaching and learning that all college professors should be asking. They force us to reconsider old questions, reevaluate our assumptions, and reexamine the foundations of what we believe, especially when they are questionable or wrong. Consider an essay from *The Neuroscience of Adult Learning*, in which cognitive scientists Louis Cozolino and Susan Sprokay casually write: "Western science, philosophy, and education share a fundamental conception of the thinker as solitary rather than embedded within a human community. This has led to a focus on technical and abstract exploration of scientific conundra [sic] rather than exploration of lived experiences and human interactions."[11]

This is simply not true. If anything, it is a modern idea, traceable back to the Enlightenment. Unfortunately, they use it as a premise to justify dismissing prior explanations of how people teach and learn, and to postulate their own, even when they reach the same conclusions as those who have preceded them but who have based theirs on observation and experience, anecdotal evidence, or philosophical orientation.

Anyone with even cursory knowledge of the history of education knows that the ancient Greeks emphasized the social context of learning and the communal pursuit of knowledge: Socrates through dialogue, Plato in his Academy, Aristotle through the Peripatetic method. Anyone who studies these masters, and takes them seriously, also knows that they help us to resist the easy and preferred answers. They show us alternatives worthy of consideration, and they remind us that teaching is an art inseparable from the aims of education as whole, of becoming then being, which professors must exemplify in their classrooms and in their own lives. By reading and studying their texts, taking from them what is valuable, and developing our own methods and styles of teaching, we learn how to become artists (in the classical sense of the term) who possess comprehensive understanding and a liberal outlook and who encapsulate the essence of liberal education in our own teaching. And teaching is for artists, as Aristotle reminds us (*Metaphysics*, 981^{b5}).

One thing you should keep in mind when reading the books and articles of modern scholars of teaching and learning, is that many of them seem unaware that they reiterate what's been said in some of the classic texts on teaching and pedagogy. Consider, for example, the popular book, *How People Learn: Brain, Mind, Experience, and School* (1999). Its authors make the same point that Locke and James made long ago, that people learn new knowledge and gain new understanding only in relation to what they already know and understand, whether true or false. People begin learning by discerning and comparing ideas, so teachers should get students "to differentiate their present ideas from conceptual beliefs and integrate them into those of the subject they are studying." If preconceived ideas or assumptions are not engaged, students are less likely to grasp the new ideas that teachers introduce. They might memorize facts or ideas for an exam, but they are not likely to stick; what's worse, students will revert to their preexisting notions, unlearning what they have memorized. Thus a critical feature of effective teaching is to prepare students' minds to receive new knowledge by relating it to previous conceptions (or even misconceptions), and then to challenge those conceptions and build a new understating as opportunities arise.

The authors of *How People Learn* also reiterate what Locke and James have already taught us, that people remember things because they have established meaningful patterns of information in their minds. Knowledge is accumulated and understanding developed through habitual forms of association. To say that a person understands something means that he or she is able to turn facts and information into usable knowledge, or convert facts into truth. Experts know more about their subjects, but they also know how to place information into relevant categories because they have developed "original conceptual structure or schemes that guide how problems are represented and understood." They learn and process new information related to their subjects faster than beginners because they are capable of seeing and making connections (patterns, relationships, or discrepancies, call them what you will). They may be good thinkers and smart people, but they also know how to draw on a "richly structured information base," which is readily available to them to explain something, to make arguments, and to act. In other words, having made appropriate connections and established patterns of thought in their minds, they have "fluent retrieval" of information.

Therefore, to get students to learn something new, teachers must pay attention to their students' beliefs, to their complete or incomplete understandings, to their prejudices and assumptions. If these are ignored, students are likely to develop different associations—and hence, a different understanding—from what teachers intend. The implication of this is worth noting. If new knowledge can only be acquired by building on old knowledge, opinions, or beliefs, and if the act of learning depends upon these as well, teachers must pay attention to these tendencies so that they can guide their students in the right direction. But this is exactly what Plato, Rousseau, and James have already said, as I have shown above, that it is necessary for teachers to understand the natures of the young and ferret out what they already know. Stimulating thought and creating the appropriate response is just another way of getting students to form new patterns of thinking and organize ideas so that they remember what they are taught.

Another thing you should keep in mind when reading the books and articles of modern scholars of teaching and learning, is that they typically work from the same premises and they share similar assumptions, chiefly the belief that anything from the pre-scientific era is irrelevant to our society and times. Consider another recent book, Carolyn Lieberg's *Teaching Your First College Class: A Practical Guide for New Faculty and Graduate Student Instructors* (Stylus Publishing, 2008).[12] Lieberg writes that it is important to help students understand what it means to be educated. "One of your challenges is to guide students away from that attitude [that college is a series of classes] toward one where they see themselves as educated adults who take pleasure in their accumulating knowledge and broadening undertakings." So far so good, but the author leaves us hanging with some vague notion that a "liberal education is, among other things, about a wide and deep understanding of the world. Helping students find ways to organize their thinking is a worthy teaching goal." There is no discussion of what that means, what those "other things" are, and how the methods she elaborates in the rest of the book will promote them—not to mention that her definition of liberal education raises all sorts of unanswered questions.

Furthermore, her "major figures in pedagogy" go no further back than John Dewey (AD 1859–1952), Lev Vygotsky (AD 1896–1934), and Benjamin Bloom (AD 1913–1999). In fact, we are told that Dewey is the "grandfather of pedagogy" whose "fame as an important thinker spread out into the wider public mind because he wrote for popular intellectual magazines on issues such as women's suffrage and the unionization of teachers." It also becomes clear that, like other modern scholars of teaching and learning, she prefers Dewey because of his constructivist views; she prefers Vygotsky because he advocated the connections between higher-order thinking and social interactions, or so-called collaborative learning, and education as a process through which students create their own meanings; and she clings to the theories of Bloom, whose taxonomy of learning domains (cognitive, affective, and psychomotor) has become a staple for modern scholars of teaching and learning and remains essentially unchallenged as the model for modern pedagogy.

There's only one reference in Lieber's book to William James (a single quotation taken from another source), and no mention of other "major figures," such as Rousseau, Locke, Aristotle, or Plato, whom most scholars of the history and philosophy of education would consider the grandfather of pedagogy. Lieber speaks, as Thoreau once observed, "as if the study of the classics would at length make way for more modern and practical studies," and added: "We might as well omit to study Nature because she is old." Yes, the classics might be interesting or quaint, a famous scholar of teaching and learning said to me, but they do not incorporate the latest methods and therefore cannot possibly be useful, reliable, or even true.

This is clearly the view of Carl Wiemanin (physicist and Nobel Prize recipient turned scholar of teaching and learning) in his essay, "Why Not Try A Scientific Approach to Scientific Education."[13] Wieman's concern is exclusively science—or rather, the teaching of science to undergraduates—through which he hopes to produce "a more scientifically literate populace to address the global challenges that humanity now faces," but which "only science can explain and possibly imagine." Therefore, he accepts only the "practices and conclusions" of the latest educational and cognitive research because they are "based on objective data rather than anecdote or tradition." He understands that "a successful science education transforms how students think." As experts, teachers of science "have lots of factual knowledge about their subjects," they have "mental organizational structures that facilitates the retrieval and effective application of their knowledge," and they "have an ability to monitor their own thinking."

Wieman further understands that, because "new ways of thinking are always built on the prior thinking of the individual," it is necessary for teachers "to take that prior thinking into account." They can make this happen in the classroom only by knowing "where the students are starting from in their thinking, so they can build on that foundation," finding "activities that ensure that the students actively think about and process the important ideas of the discipline," and having "mechanisms by which they probe and then guide that thinking on an ongoing basis." In short, learning improves when teachers engage students, monitor their thinking, and provide adequate feedback.

Under closer scrutiny, however, there's really nothing new or strictly "scientific" about Wieman's approach. In fact, you might even have noticed that he is espousing some of the same principles of teaching and learning that have been stated in the classic texts on education and pedagogy, as we've seen above. What's more, he takes away from science teachers the act of discovery (which is the essence of his own message) by reading those texts themselves. In my view, his article would have been more illuminating if he related the activity of teaching science to the aims of liberal education as a whole, and if he showed show teachers how understanding the process of thinking develops the habits of mind essential to the liberally educated person: for example, how it develops skepticism because it get students to doubt their existing opinions, assumptions, and beliefs—which should be clear to them so that they can acquire new knowledge; how it develops discipline because it forces students to consider and attend to new ideas that challenge or substantiate the old; and how it develops judgment because it gets students to discern and compare information and select what is relevant, useful, or true.

A third thing you should keep in mind when reading modern scholarship of teaching and learning, is that even cognitive scientists will tell you that cognitive science is not a definitive roadmap to effective teaching. For example, in discussing the amygdala, the part of the brain that plays a primary role in the processing and memory of emotional reactions, James Zull writes that students who are more involved in their work "feel *less* nervous and afraid."[14] Therefore, by focusing on "the work itself rather than the extrinsic reward, the intrinsic reward systems can begin to engage." When this happens, students are engaging in active learning. But, he adds, the "*postulated* connection between the basal structures of the front brain and pleasure leads to an interesting *prediction* about passive versus active learning. Specifically, any learning that involves some sense of progress and control by the learner *might* be expected to engage the basal structures. This would be learning that is pleasurable. On the other hand, learning that involves recall of associations would be more connected with the back part of the cerebral cortex, the receiving part of the brain. This learning *might* be less pleasurable and require more effort" (italics added). At bottom, Zull tells us, effective teaching is ultimately "a question of philosophy for the teacher."

These remarks are consistent with what he writes in *The Neuroscience of Adult Learning*, that the "neurological nature of learning *strongly suggests* that there is no age finality for any learning," adding that no matter how "widely accepted" our understanding of the biological properties of the brain may be, "all current theories will automatically be reconsidered and revisited as our knowledge about the brain continues to grow." In a similar vein the editors of this book dismiss "observation and experience, anecdotal evidence, and philosophical orientation" to inform the practice of teaching and learning, but they also admit that, although neuroscientists can "trace pathways of the brain involved in various learning tasks," they can only at best "*infer* which learning environments are *most likely* to be effective." The editors also point out that there has been "conflicting guidance" from "psychological theories and sociological analysis, which attempt to describe what learning is and how it takes place." Pat Wolfe, another contributor to the volume, reminds us that only a few decades ago scientists were telling educators that behavior is the basis of all learning: They "determined whether individuals had learned something by observing their performance," and they explained learning "in terms of stimulus and response; emphasis was on acquisition and manipulation of information."[15] In other words, basing our approach to teaching exclusively on the premises of modern science might not be as definite or sound as some would like us to believe. It seems that effective teaching is a question of philosophy after all.

If there is one lesson from modern cognitive research that we should pay especial attention to, it's that expertise and specialization can hinder both teaching and the act of learning. Professors with the most knowledge are not always the best teachers. Experts and specialists—who have ideas fixed in their memories, which are readily retrievable; and who already rely on multiple cues to trigger the associations of understanding—often fail to notice what is easy and what is difficult for their students to learn. It is precisely because they have developed the appropriate habits of thought and mind, and the proper conceptual framework, that they can perform what they are doing easily and without struggling to think about it. But what they fail to realize is that they often hide assumptions or obscure their subject by not revealing these assumptions to students at the right time. They begin, as Quintilian observed, where they ought to end, and through ostentatious haste, retard their students' progress by attempting to shorten the road.

So what are some ways to promote retention based on what we know about memory and learning from the discussion above? One way is simply to restore rigor to our courses and instill self-discipline in our students. Psychologist Mihaly Csikszentmihalyi (no stranger to pedagogical tradition I've been referring to here) has shown through decades of research that genuine learning is more likely to take place when people are engaged in activities that are challenging and complex and that enable them to organize consciousness and prevent intellectual entropy. They must take on tasks they have a chance of completing, they must concentrate on what they do, and they must have clear goals and receive immediate feedback.[16] As teachers we must emphasize and reinforce that intellectual pursuits require as much rigor and training as athletics. The analogy must be pressed, writes Jacques Barzun, that "in the exercise of intellect those who lack the muscles, coordination, and will power can claim no place on the training table, let alone on the playing field."[17] Discipline and drill are necessary, but that doesn't mean rote memorization, although some repetition is necessary for memory to occur, as William James reminds us: "*No reception without reaction, no impression with correlative expression*—this is the great maxim which the teacher ought never to forget." But repetition must never become mechanical or dull the mind. The real reason students lack motivation and don't remember what they learn is that they are simply not interested what they are being taught.

Another way to promote retention is to reinforce ideas in a variety of contexts using a variety of examples to illustrate a point or explain their significance. William James again: "The difference between an interesting and a tedious teacher consists in little more than the inventiveness by which the one is able to mediate these associations and connections." The "law of native interests" dictates that "any object not interesting in itself may become interesting through becoming associated with an object in which an interest already exists." Associate something less interesting with something more interesting and the "two associated objects grow together as the interesting portion sheds its quality over the whole." James calls this "borrowing an interest," in which the new thing "becomes as real and as strong as that of any natively interesting thing." Far from impoverishing the original, it makes it even more interesting. Through adequate preparation—thinking of appropriate anecdotes, reminiscences, even stories that are useful in weaving together what's old with what's new—will teachers be able effectively to correlate the old with the new and connect various subjects.[18]

Yet another way to promote retention is through common or communal learning, or what Jules Romains calls unanism.[19] The theory suggests that people see themselves as individuals until a single event or emotion brings them together as a group; once this happens the group takes on its own identity and begins to live, feel, think, and act collectively. The energy and identity of the group then supersede that of any individual. It can be triggered by almost anything, whether silly, profound, or ennobling; it often occurs at sports events when the spectators are caught up in the excitement of the game and roar together as a crowd; it can take place in a meeting or during a speech when members are moved by a speaker; it can happen at a movie or in a theater when the audience share the emotions of the actors; it can even occur in a classroom when students are enraptured by an energetic teacher.

If unanism exists at all, says Gilbert Highet, it will be shared. "To create it, or to help it to come into being, is one of the teacher's main tasks. It cannot exist unless there is a rapport, a give-and-take, something like a unanimist relationship between the pupils and the teacher." The best indication that unanism exists is the atmosphere before a class begins. Are the students talking with each other and interacting, or are they sitting there silently, listening to their iPods, playing with their Blackberries or mobile phones, absorbed in themselves? The five extra minutes it takes to begin a class because students are talking is time well spent. Creating unanism, however, does not mean forcing it, but generating the sense of unity naturally among students. Whether permitting, I'll take mine outside to re-enact the Battle of Crécy, or for a walk around the campus to look at something that they probably haven't noticed; I've even taught students Yoga as an extracurricular activity, taking advantage of their gregariousness and love of play. Small activities like these help them open up and talk to each other, which they are inclined to do anyway. The aim is to promote those personal attachments that are essential to all learning.

But let's be clear about one thing: Communal learning is not the same thing as "group work" or "collaborative" learning, which modern scholars of teaching and learning, particularly those under the influence of Vygotsky, love. In theory, group work should promote communal learning; in practice, it often creates a false sense of unity (even disunity) among students because it reinforces their feeling that education is an unnatural and artificial activity, that they are learning for school, not for life, as Seneca says. The one collective emotion that group work almost certainly engenders is resentment. Good students resent being forced to work with indifferent and weak students who take advantage of them; indifferent students resent group work because they are forced to do something they don't want to do anyway (but at least they get to sponge off the good students); perhaps the only students who like group work are the weak ones because it promotes safety in numbers.

Another danger of group work is that it does little to promote self-knowledge and the habits of thought and mind that are essential to liberal education. "Listening to one another, students sometimes change their opinions," writes Professor Mark Edmundson of the University of Virginia, but what they generally can't do "is acquire a new vocabulary, a new perspective, that will cast issues in a fresh light."[20] They must have their ideas driven back by continuous questioning; their minds must be turned upside down through engaging lectures and discussions, which they also can't do. Many scholars of teaching and learning naïvely assume that students can somehow teach themselves, or learn from each other. But just think about "how many centuries it would take the student to rediscover by himself all mathematics and science developed since Pythagoras," as Jacques Barzun has pointed out. It's like signing up for a dance class only to have the instructor play some music and say, "Now dance."

Another danger of group work almost never mentioned by its proponents is how it can "annul the individual, suppress individual intelligence, and reinforce the belief that the group is always right," as Gilbert Highet reminds us. We do a great disservice to students by inflating their hopes and making them think that they are as capable of performing as the next person. I don't deny that some group work can be effective, as Alexander Astin suggests: The "student's peer group is the single most potent source of influence on growth and development during the undergraduate years;" but it is not as effective as the advocates of collaborative learning would have us believe, as Arum and Roksa have shown: "All hours studying are not the same: studying alone is beneficial, but studying with peers is not."[21] Don't force it. If students are connected, they will study together naturally or work in groups on their own.

Instruction is always superior to discovery in undergraduate education because, as Aquinas reminds us, a "teacher who knows the whole science explicitly can teach it to a pupil more readily than the pupil himself could learn it from his own rather general knowledge of the principles of the science." Carl Wieman reiterates Aquinas' point when he writes that the essence of effective teaching is to get "students engaged in thinking deeply about the subject at an appropriate level and then monitoring that thinking and guiding it to be more expert-like." Even cognitive scientists James Zull and Daniel Willingham suggest that teachers must use discovery learning cautiously.[22]

Teachers are capable of learning on their own, having demonstrated their knowledge and mastery of a tradition to the satisfaction of their teachers, who once guided them in the act of discovery. Effective teachers continue to learn through discovery, that is, through scholarship and teaching, which is "the highest form of study," according to Mark Van Doren. The act of learning will always be aided discovery (i.e., instruction) until they have proven that they can learn on their own. At that point, they should be awarded their degrees and sent on their way.

CHAPTER 3

SPEAK, THAT I MAY SEE THEE

If a man's got no audience—why then, it's of no use to go on lecturing.

~ Chaucer, *The Canterbury Tales*

I feel sorry for flight attendants. I think the worst part of their job is before takeoff, when the plane is leaving the terminal and they are reviewing its safety features, which includes showing passengers how to buckle their seat belts. Yeah, right. I feel sorry for them because everybody ignores them, except me. Now I admit, I'm not really *listening* to them. I know how to buckle my seat belt—after all, I was a paratrooper in the army and I've flown so many times that I could probably go over the safety features of almost any airplane. No, I only appear to be listening because I know what it's like to speak before a group of people who are clearly not listening—as when I have given a bad lecture. It's why I still get nervous every time I enter a classroom. It's not because I don't have much experience in front of students, it's the anticipation and fear—yes, fear—that my class will be flat. Nothing terrifies me more.

Lecturing gets a bad rap these days because it is said to make students passive. But critics miss the point. If that were true, students wouldn't learn from various media—television, music, and movies, for example—which require no interaction at all. The difference is that students find what they watch and listen to in these media interesting but most lectures boring.

The Skinny on Teaching: What You Don't Learn in Graduate School, pp. 33–43
Copyright © 2011 by Information Age Publishing
All rights of reproduction in any form reserved.

Most teaching is done by explaining what is vague and unknown, but most teachers never learn or practice how to speak effectively and instruct orally. As a result, they don't know how to lecture. The fault is not with the method, but with lecturers, who do not know how to stimulate thought through speech and obtain the required response or reaction in students. By lecturing I do not mean not "lecturing at," the stereotypical image of the professor standing before a class spewing out facts (Ben Stein in *Ferris Bueller's Day Off* comes to mind: "Anyone? ... Anyone?"); I mean instructive speech that promotes learning. When done well, it is a useful and effective mode of instruction because it gives and explains information, it gets students to think in ways they have not thought before, it fills in gaps in knowledge, and it cultivates understanding by correcting wrong impressions.

A good lecture will have at least three effects.[1] First, it will convince students that the theme is of first-rate importance, arousing curiosity and driving them to investigate the subject further on their own. Some teachers are born with the ability to inspire this kind of enthusiasm in their students; others show mastery of the art of generalization that is one sign of an educated mind. The best lectures not only stimulate curiosity—which Samuel Johnson writes is one of the "characteristics of a vigorous intellect"—they make students believe they are on to something big, compelling them to find out more as if their lives depended on it. Allan Bloom was said to have this effect on his students. When he lectured, writes his former student Clifford Orwin, "time stopped, and one felt oneself wafted to a higher plane of life and thought." He made students *feel* as if study was something exalted, "in a manner in which only feeling is believable."[2] Most of us need to work at arousing this kind of enthusiasm in our students, but it encapsulates the essence of effective teaching, as William James observed: "you must work your pupil into such a state of interest in what you are going to teach him, that every other subject of attention is banished from his mind; then reveal it to him so impressively that he will remember the occasion to his dying day; and finally fill him with devouring curiosity to know what the next steps in connection to the subject are."

Second, a good lecture must impart genuinely new knowledge or a new point of view not obtainable in textbooks, from the Internet, or from the other obvious sources. Unfortunately, most lectures reproduce information or summarize knowledge to save students the effort and time of reading for themselves. A common tactic, especially with new teachers, is to piece together information from textbooks. I knew a teacher who took pride in compiling her lectures from six different ones! Of course, if her graduate program had prepared her to teach she would have mastered all the necessary sources and formulated her own thoughts on the subject. Instead she became a tertiary source (not merely a secondary source), removing herself and her students even further from the essence of their subject. This encourages laziness, not only in students, but also among teachers, who set a bad example when they fail to demonstrate a higher level of understanding or the ability to offer a new perspective on a topic. Thus the third requirement of a good lecture, that it should "raise new problems upon old material which force students to think out for themselves the way and the nature of their solution," as Harold Laski says. It should, in short, illustrate some new connection that isn't obvious to students.

A good lecture produces understanding (or reduces misunderstanding) through speech. It will sustain the attention of students if it is clear and if it conveys a teacher's exact meaning, which might mean being explicit or pointing out what seems obvious to us. Words must refer to things, and they should be ordinary, specific, and concrete. They should never hide emptiness of thought, ambiguities and uncertainty, or confusion in the teacher's mind. As Montaigne suggests, the closer one's language is to ordinary life, the better: "The speech I love is a simple, natural speech, the same on paper as in the mouth; a speech succulent and sinewy, brief and compressed, not so much dainty and well-combed as vehement and brusque ... rather difficult than boring, remote from affection, irregular, disconnected and bold; each bit making a body in itself; not pedantic, not monkish, not lawyer-like, but rather soldierly."[3]

If only Governor Bobby Jindal of Louisiana had listened to Montaigne, his response to President Obama's first address to a joint session of Congress in February 2009 might not have been so awful. But it was, and that's because his speech came across as unnatural, according to acting coach Howard Fine.[4] His words never seemed to emanate from himself. His examples seemed disconnected from his own experiences and from what he said. He locked himself into a "false demeanor" and appeared artificial, stilted, and stiff—like many professors when they lecture (remember the student I mentioned earlier?). Natural speech is always more persuasive because it expresses the speaker's emotions and character, what is known in classical rhetoric as *ethos*.[5]

Indifference is deadly for teachers, who must engender interest in what they are saying by establishing their *ethos* with the audience. Teaching is as much emotional as intellectual, and students are more likely to learn from teachers who are animated and visibly excited about their subject.[6] This means affecting the emotions and passions of students, what classical rhetoric calls *pathos*, as much as it means reaching their minds. Lectures might be well arranged (*taxis*), they might be logical (*logos*), and they might use the appropriate language, vocabulary, and style (*lexis*), but they also will be merely dull recitations if those giving them do not establish their character or put students put in the right frame of mind. Plato has condensed the essence of effective speaking in this short passage from *Phaedrus*:

> First, you must know the truth concerning everything you are speaking or writing about; you must learn how to define each thing in itself; and, having

defined it, you must know how to divide it into kinds until you reach something indivisible. Second, you must understand the nature of the soul, along the same lines; you must determine which kind of speech is appropriate to each kind of soul, prepare and arrange your speech accordingly, and offer a complex and elaborate speech to a complex and elaborate soul and a simple speech to a simple one. Then, and only then, will you be able to use speech artfully, to the extent that its nature allows it to be used that way, either in order to teach or in order to persuade.[7]

People are not only persuaded when a thing has been demonstrated to them, adds Aristotle (*Rhetoric*, Book 1), they are also persuaded when they feel their interests are involved or at stake. Teachers who establish their *ethos* and stir students' *pathos* are more likely to generate intellectual excitement than those who are oblivious to their audience and drone on and on and on ("Anyone? ... Anyone?").

Another way to fail to gain and hold your students' attention is to talk down to them. It is much better to risk talking over their heads—after all, the point of a good lecture is to get them to stretch their minds and increase their knowledge—but one should never go too far over their heads and risk losing them. For instance, my use of Descartes' *Discourse on Method* when teaching the Scientific Revolution also gives me an opportunity to raise larger philosophical and epistemological issues with my students. In addition to asking them what Descartes is saying, I solicit objections to his arguments or question the validity of his first principle by asking: What does he mean by accept nothing as true except that which "was presented to my mind so *clearly and distinctly* as to exclude all grounds of doubt?" From there I ask additional questions: How does he *know* that something is *clear and distinct*? Is his answer, "I think, therefore I am," sufficient to eliminate all doubt about our ability to know anything? What if we are brains in vats? What does this do to "objective" truth or understanding? And so on. Many students have seen the movie *The Matrix*, which helps to illustrate my point, but after dangling these questions before them for a while, I usually begin to notice eyes glazing over, or frustration or even exasperation setting in, and so turn the discussion back to the concrete matter of Descartes' method. But I have gotten students to see that, although they might be able to explain what Descartes means by deduction, we have only scratched the surface and there is still more to consider. For a similar reason, classes that exceed the typical comfort zone of about thirty minutes to an hour should include other activities or exercises.

At all costs, never read an entire lecture from your notes or a PowerPoint presentation. I never understood the point. Why not photocopy it or post it online and let students read it themselves? Reading a lecture suggests that a professor doesn't know his or her subject well enough to talk about it without a script. Does the expert mechanic need notes to fix a car? The surgeon in the operating room? The actor on stage? Why should teachers if they are experts in their subjects? As an undergraduate, I always thought it was hypocritical that professors could use notes when they lectured but would not allow me and fellow students to use them during exams. Notes are essential for preparation—reading the primary sources, organizing thoughts, and writing up the lecture—but one should avoid appearing scripted, which is a sure way to disengage students. Lecturing will always be more effective if teachers appear natural in the classroom, having prepared, organized, and rehearsed their lectures beforehand.

Teachers could learn a great deal from actors. Good actors know how to deliver a monologue and enrapture an audience, while teachers delivering lectures, also a kind of monologue, often have difficulty keeping students' attention. The chief difference is drama, which is present on stage but often missing in the classroom. Without drama, little genuine learning takes place, and students are less likely to be drawn into the act of discovery. Instead they will simply take notes, stuff their memories for the exam, and forget everything afterwards. A person can learn just about anything from books at home, says Cardinal Newman, but "the detail, the color, the tone, the air, the life which makes it live in us" can be caught only from those in whom it lives already. To become "exact and fully furnished in any subject of teaching which is diversified and complicated," he adds, one "must consult the living man and listen to his living voice."[8]

Once more modern studies affirm what a great thinker has already taught us. Newman's claim is supported by Daniel T. Willingham (and other cognitive scientists) who have demonstrated that narrative is more effective in getting people to remember things because stories are "psychologically privileged."[9] People find stories "interesting, easy to understand, and easy to remember," writes Willingham, and therefore generally treat them differently from other types of material. Great oral storytellers—whether Charles Dickens in the nineteenth century or Garrison Keillor today—know how to make a subject so concrete that it becomes convincing and unforgettable. One reason is that stories move along and change, which both John Locke and William James said is the key to keeping the attention focused; another reason is that stories are structured around causality, conflict, and complications, which make them easier to remember. Causality "is so powerful a cue to recall," writes Willingham, "that subjects will use it even in expository prose, if it's available."

Unfortunately, many academics look down on narrative, in writing as well as in lecturing, and therefore miss a crucial opportunity to connect with their audience. Mark Edmundson of the University of Virginia states, rather proudly, "I don't teach to amuse, to divert, or even, for that matter, to be merely interesting."[10] The qualifier "merely" is telling. He apparently thinks, like many professors, that he is interesting, or that his subject is interesting, because it is interesting to him. But Edmundson and others like him ignore that they can teach their students only if they attract and hold their attention. Adding suspense and surprise to lectures, rather than teaching as if the world were logical and predictable, is more likely to elicit the appropriate physical and emotional responses in students, help stave off boredom, and stimulate the desired reaction.[11]

"The lecture room is the one place where drama properly becomes theater," writes Jacques Barzun, and teachers should learn from actors because they have much in common when practicing their art: Both use captive devices to hold the attention of their audience; and both must always seem fresh.[12] A good lecture, like a good performance, will always appear as if it's being given for the first time, heightening the sense of novelty by dramatizing the moments of discovery. Great teachers are able to transform themselves before their students: When teaching St. Augustine, they are pious Christians; when teaching Locke, good bourgeoisie; when teaching Marx, avid communists and atheists. Teachers who understand the importance of drama in the classroom often develop a "teacher-self" by acting a part or performing a role, as one finds in theatre, and by showing "verve, color, humor, creativity, surprise."[13]

Dramatic lecturing takes a fluent speaker who neither uses notes nor is shy about effects; it requires emphasis, timing, and organization—even humor, props, and role-playing. At Syracuse University, when I was a teaching assistant, Professor Kenneth Pennington would dress up and give a monologue as Peter Abelard when he talked about the philosopher's life and times. It was not beneath this world-class scholar to don a costume and play the part. From him I got the idea of taking students outside to re-enact the Battle of Crécy. And although one should never read an entire lecture, for the reasons mentioned above, notes can occasionally be used as an effective prop. Sometimes I stand before my students with a page in hand and read lengthy quotations or statistics while gesturing; sometimes I deliberately consult my notes to look up a fact or appear as if I need them to put myself back on track when the discussion has taken a detour; sometimes I script jokes and gestures into my lectures, a tactic I learned from studying the oratory of Winston Churchill.

Perhaps teachers such as Edmundson will say that these measures are unnecessary or extreme, but already we play roles every day and use props in the classroom, whether drawing diagrams on a blackboard or projecting a PowerPoint presentation. Properly used, technology is a wonderful prop that should be available in every classroom. For instance, I create web sites for all of my courses and use them to facilitate my lectures. I show maps, images, portraits of people I am discussing; I post quotations from primary sources so that students can follow what I am reading; sometimes I have students read the quotations aloud and then analyze them. If I must dwell on a point for some time, I often show images related to the topic, not to distract them, but to hold their attention through a sense of movement, since no unvarying object can hold the mind for long. I use a remote mouse with my Internet hookup so that I can walk up and down the aisles and interact with students. "The genius of the interesting teacher," says William James, "consists in sympathetic divination of the sort of material with which the pupil's mind is likely to be spontaneously engaged—and in the ingenuity which discovers paths of connection from the material to matters to be newly learned."[14] Properly used, technology makes teaching vivid; it can make abstract subjects concrete and therefore more memorable and relevant; and it is a medium that students understand, like to use, and learn from.

However, technology can never replace living teachers, who should be animated and highly expressive both in their voice and in their bodily movements. "It is not enough to show what we ought to say," again says Aristotle (*Rhetoric*, Book 3), "we must also say it as we ought" and "work toward producing the right impression of a speaker."[15] We must know, in other words, how to deliver our message. Delivery ... Delivery ... Delivery. Everything comes down to delivery, or the right manner and management of public speaking. Just as a polished speaker "knows how to temper, to vary, and to arrange the several parts of speech," writes Quintilian, "so in delivery he knows how to adapt his action to every variety of complexion he utters."

Teachers spend most of their time in the classroom talking and explaining, but how many have ever trained their voices or their bodies? How many pay attention to the rhythms of their sentences and the lengths of words? How many find ways to keep and drive a passage through without rushing? How many practice speaking loudly or softly, or with a high or a low pitch? How many know how to vary their manner to suit the subject at hand? Trained speakers modulate their voices and regulate their speed of speaking. For instance, they deliver salient points slowly and emphatically, and the connecting arguments in a more conversational tone; they punctuate their voices by pausing, adding variety to their manner of speaking. The raising or lowering or other inflexion of the voice accordingly tends to move the feelings of the hearers. "The most effective fact in oratory," said G. K. Chesterton, who knew a thing or two about the subject, "is an unexpected change in the voice."[16] In short, they know how to use their voices and their bodies to convey their message and avoid monotony.

Acting coach Cicely Berry writes that voice is a personal statement through which "you convey your precise thought and feelings."[17] She advocates opening up the voice's possibilities by doing exercises for relaxation and breathing, by increasing the muscularity of the lips and tongue, and by changing one's standards and expectations. Just as we build our vocabulary so that we can choose the exact words to convey our precise meaning, we should exercise our voices to convey our meaning accurately. Berry lists four traits that affect the responsiveness and efficiency of the voice. The first is *environment*, because we learn to speak like those around us; the second is *ear*, or the ability to perceive of sound; the third is *physical agility*, because the degree of speech depends on muscular awareness and use; the fourth is *personality*, or the individual traits that express one's physical and psychological state. Trained actors know how to manage these traits, whereas untrained speakers often "push the energy" from within and force emotion and feeling. For instance, anxiety and tension waste energy, which in turn interferes with a speaker's pronunciation and volume and is more likely to cause an audience to recoil. "In real life," Berry observes, "you step back from the person who is over-anxious, over-enthusiastic, the person who gets you in a corner when he talks to you, and it is the same with the actor's relationship with his audience." Effective speakers find "the right balance in the voice" among clarity, pleasure, euphony, variation, and credibility.

Delivery also means finding the right manner and management of the body, because as St. Augustine correctly observed, only "a very small measure of what a speaker thinks is expressed in his words."[18] Teachers, again like actors, need to know how to use the physical animation of their bodies—facial expressions, gestures, postures, movement, eye contact—in short, all the modes of nonverbal expression. They should train their bodies to gain the attention of their students and keep them focused on their message, lest they "lose the house" as the actors call it and break the bond between them and their students. This can be something as simple as knowing how to guide them by maintaining eye-contact or changing one's posture during dull or unexciting parts. Listeners typically "put more faith in a speaker's nonverbal message than the verbal," writes Michael Chekov, who suggests that we pay attention to the constant interplay between the human body and psychology—and who reiterates what Montaigne taught us about body language long ago: "Every movement reveals us."[19]

Acting coach Howard Fine also reminds us that true emotion travels and "is reflected in body language and in the voice." In assessing Governor Jindal's response to President Obama, he points out that viewers could sense the "hollowness" of his prepared speech by simply looking in his eyes and listening to his voice. Jindal did not vary his pitch, and he barely changed his expression. When he tried to add variety to his manner it seemed "predetermined for emphasis and to give the impression of a real expression." Even worse, he seemed coached on "where to pause and what words to stress." In short, everything he did seemed fabricated and insincere. On the other hand, Obama is effective as a speaker because he is organic and "in the moment" and "connects his real feelings to what he is saying." For that reason he "comes across as the real deal."[20]

Chekov recommends training the body as an effective instrument of creative expression, which he calls *radiation*. To radiate is to give or to send out—the opposite of receiving or reception—although in acting and teaching there is a constant exchange of the two. Passive actors and teachers risk creating a psychological vacuum and weakening the audience's attention; imaginative actors and teachers, aware of the interaction between physical bodies and psychological gestures, radiate the realm of their feelings—ease, form, beauty, entirety—and move beyond the monotony of mannerisms. The "actor in the truest sense," says Chekov, is "a being who is endowed with the ability to see and experience things which are obscure to the average person." We might also say that the "teacher in the truest sense" likewise interprets life itself. Both actors and teachers convey what they see and feel; therefore, both must be able to use their bodies to convey their impressions from within.[21]

In sum, delivery is essential for conveying one's message while lecturing and for eliciting the appropriate physical and emotional reaction in one's students during a lecture. It means evoking prompt and ready responses from them, adding variety, employing recapitulations, illustrations, examples, novelty of order, and breaking up routine. Teachers who are lively and alert are more likely to affect students through their example than those who are not.[22] If abstract, they will show the nature of their subject with concrete examples; if discussing something unfamiliar, they will trace it by making analogies with what students know; if dealing with an inanimate topic, they will enliven it through a story. They know how to elicit interest in the subject from within by the warmth with which they care for their topic. They use variety in their voices, their gestures, and in their overall manner of speaking. In fine, they understand that they make an impression every time they step in the classroom—by their speech, by theirs manners, even by their clothes.

Yes, clothes. If few teachers think about the effect of voice and bodily movements on teaching, even fewer, I imagine, think about the effect of their clothes. Clothes are "nothing less than the furniture of the mind made visible," James Laver wrote some time ago.[23] They convey information about us—our occupation, social origins, economic class, personality, opinions, current mood. Alison Lurie calls clothes a "universal tongue," a form of nonverbal communication, a language of signs, which people choose to define and describe themselves. "In language we distinguish between someone who speaks a sentence well—clearly, and with confidence and dignity—and someone who speaks it badly." Likewise, in dress the manner is important because we judge the fitness of the garment. Is it too big or too small or just right? No one is actually indifferent to the way he or she dresses. "Even those who seem not to care whether their garments are in fashion or not, or eccentric in style," writes Lawrence Langer, "really achieve a feeling of superiority because of the fact that they are shockingly unconcerned."[24] Teachers should think of their clothes as another form of nonverbal expression, an extension of personality, "For the apparel doth proclaim the man" (Shakespeare, *Hamlet*, 1.3.72).

I hear the objections. "The way I dress is no one's business. I am here to teach students, not participate in a fashion show. My authority comes from what I teach, not the way I dress." True, but it is also true that clothes can detract from one's authority in the classroom. Like speech, behavior, even cleanliness, for example, they are a sign of respectability, or at least of self-respect. We wear professional attire to job interviews, not only because it is appropriate, but because we want to make a good impression on our prospective colleagues. We avoid inappropriate speech and behavior in the classroom, so why should we accept an inappropriate appearance? Professor Pennington always wore a suit when he taught (when he wasn't dressing up like Abelard) to distinguish himself from his students. I'm not advocating snobbery, or suggesting some kind of dress-for-success strategy, or even a dress code; I am suggesting that teachers should pay attention to their appearance, not only because it makes a statement about themselves, but also because, and more importantly, students pay attention to what their teachers wear and draw conclusions about them based on it. For better or worse, clothes reinforce the impression we give our students about our subject and ourselves. I know Thoreau says in *Walden* (Chapter 1), "beware of all enterprises that require new clothes," but this time he was wrong.

Perhaps clothes should be thought of as a costume that adds to the classroom environment. Atmosphere, says Chekov, is the heart, the feelings, the soul of every piece of art. It must prevail over individual feelings and affect the three psychological functions of people—their thoughts, feelings, and will impulses; it must deepen the perception of spectators and create reciprocal action between the actor and his audience. Teachers who establish the desired relationship between themselves and their students will be more expressive; they can use atmosphere to emphasize important points or ideas. In short, knowing how to use classroom space and its limitations can inspire learning by reinforcing the bond between teachers and their students; not knowing how to use it (or ignoring it altogether) can stifle learning by widening the psychologically void space between them.

Another way to "lose the house" is to disrupt the flow or dramatic effect of a lecture by stopping to rearrange the set. Every chair, desk, or board—that is, every prop—should be prearranged to meet your needs, which may mean getting to class early to set up. In theater, this is called *proxemics*, or the effect that spatial distances between individuals have on the performance. Proxemics establishes the relationship between students and teachers in the classroom as much as the relationship between an audience and the actors on stage. Is the sight line blocked? What movement around the classroom will best convey certain points? Where are students sitting? Students in front or within the direct sight of the professor tend to be more attentive and responsive than those in back. In large lecture halls, I impose a five-row rule (or a six- or an eight-), depending on the number of students. Students must sit within the assigned rows because I refuse to address a scattered audience and try to make appropriate use of my space. We must try to make the classroom or lecture hall—our stage—fit the course. I realize that this is often beyond our control, we do not always get to pick our classrooms, but there are some things that we can do to create the appropriate atmosphere.

Lecturing is one mode of oral instruction that promotes learning. It should never be just spewing out facts or tidbits of information, but a way of getting students to cultivate habits of thought and mind. When done well, it promotes genuine *synergy of learning* by encouraging students to pay attention, copy accurately, follow an argument, detect ambiguities or false inference, test guesses by summoning up contrary instances, organize their time and their thought for study—all these arts, writes Jacques Barzun, "cannot be taught in the air but only through the difficulties of a defined subject; they cannot be taught in one course or in 1 year, but must be acquired gradually in dozens of connections."[25] Lecturing is a part of the conversation—the formative process of higher education—that aims to convince students of a subject's importance, impart genuinely new knowledge, and change students' minds. When done properly, it is an effective mode of instruction because it generates understanding, encourages students to think on their own, and promotes learning, despite what critics say.

CHAPTER 4

A LITTLE MORE CONVERSATION

We flee from correction; we should face it and go to meet it, especially when it comes in the form of discussion, not ex cathedra.

~ Montaigne, *"Of the art of discussion"*

Academics don't agree on many things, but almost all of them believe that students must develop critical thinking. "The chief way in which the student learns to think," suggests Harold Laski, "is by testing his mind against the teacher's mind. He must learn to ask significant questions and to explain to himself significant answers." Modern cognitive scientists agree, as Derek Bok has noted, adding that teachers must "create a process of active learning by posing problems, challenging student answers, and members of the class to apply information and concepts in assigned readings to a variety of new situations."[1] Of course, lectures alone are insufficient to achieve them. They must be supplemented with written work, examinations, and classroom discussions. Especially classroom discussions. Lots of them.

Typically only first-rate and mature minds gain anything from lectures, and average students need consistent personal contact. "That means that the discussion class must be small and the teacher of first-rate quality," writes Laski again; it also means that lower-level teaching should be done by professors, not by teaching assistants, who are half-baked at best. Even large

---

The Skinny on Teaching: What You Don't Learn in Graduate School, pp. 45–57
Copyright © 2011 by Information Age Publishing
All rights of reproduction in any form reserved.

introductory courses must incorporate informal discussions. All my courses, including those which have had as many as 50 students, are centered around them. They are effective because they are the most natural and organic method of instruction for teachers, and because they engage students and promote genuine learning among them.

To this day, no scholar of teaching and learning has devised a better or more sound method of oral instruction than the Socratic method. It is still superior to all others because it facilitates the exchange of ideas and it gets students to participate actively in events as they unfold, as John Comenius wrote in the sixteenth century. The "attention between question and answer, the various forms of expression and the amusing remarks that may be introduced, and even the changes that may be rung upon the *dramatis personae*" tend to counteract antipathy and create "a keen desire for further knowledge."[2] With the Socratic method both teaching and the act of learning take on the form of a conservation—a dialogue, not a monologue—which "excites and retains the attention" better than any other method of instruction.

Montaigne agreed with Comenius. Discussion, he says, is the "most fruitful and natural exercises of our mind," and a competent discussion leader is like a jouster who "presses on my flanks, prods me right and left; his ideas launch mine. Rivalry, glory, competition, push me and lift me above myself. And unison is an altogether boring quality in discussion." Through the Socratic method students stretch and test their minds because they are "strengthened by communication" with the "vigorous and orderly minds" of their teachers.[3]

Even that most modern of moderns, John Stuart Mill, writes in his *Autobiography* (Chapter 1) that the Socratic method "is unsurpassed as a discipline for correcting the errors, and clearing up the confusions incident to the *intellectus sibi permissus*, the understanding which has made up all its bundles of associations under the guidance of popular phraseology.

> The close, searching elenchus by which the man of vague generalities is constrained either to express his meaning to himself in definite terms, or to confess that he does not know what he is talking about; the perpetual testing of all general statements by particular instances; the siege in form which is laid to the meaning of large abstract terms, by fixing upon some still larger class name which includes that and more, and dividing down to the thing sought—marking out its limits and definition by a series of accurately drawn distinctions between it and each of the cognate objects which are successively parted off from it—all this, as an education for precise thinking, is inestimable.

Teachers who have mastered the art are fluid and natural in the classroom. They know how to ask the right questions to elicit responses, play devil's advocate, even create a sense of drama—like Socrates in Plato's dialogues, who knew exactly what he was going to say, where he wanted to lead the discussion, and how to get there. They display, quite simply, the mental agility of a first-rate lawyer whose qualities Francis Wellman summarizes in his fascinating (and highly recommended) book, *The Art of Cross-Examination*:

- great ingenuity;
- a habit of logical thought;
- clearness of perception in general;
- infinite patience and self-control;
- the power to read men's minds intuitively, to judge their characters by their faces, to appreciate their motives;
- the ability to act with force and precision;
- a masterful knowledge of the subject-matter itself;
- an extreme caution; and
- the *instinct to discover the weak point* in the witness under examination.[4]

Professor Edmundson of the University of Virginia rejects the Socratic method—"the animated, sometimes impolite give-and-take between student and teacher"—as "too jagged for current sensibilities." I suppose that's because some students feel intimidated or put on the spot—as if *they* were being cross-examined by their professors. But Socratic questioning is not Socratic bullying. When done right, the teacher will show intelligence and discernment, wit and vivacity, what Schopenhauer says is the essence of conversing well. A good discussion exposes weaknesses in arguments while forcing students to marshal their thoughts, argue out beliefs, and practice speaking clearly and in complete sentences. Good conversation, adds Montaigne, "is not vigorous and generous enough if it is not quarrelsome, if it is civilized and artful, if it fears knocks and moves with constraint. *For there can be no discussion without contradiction* [Cicero]." Teachers facile in the method keep their audience—their students—"always interested and on the alert," bringing out their points "so clearly that men of ordinary intelligence can understand them," as Wellman says of the expert trial lawyer.

Perhaps the real reason many teachers (and students) oppose the Socratic method as a principle means of instruction is that it requires a lot of energy and work. No doubt, the Socratic method is difficult. It demands "constant alertness, invariable good humor, complete earnestness, and utter self-surrender to the cause of truth," as Gilbert Highet reminds us.[5] Its success depends on students who have done the reading and assignments before class, who have good memories and are good learners, and who possess the appropriate disposition to learn. Its success also depends on teachers who must ensure that students are prepared *and* who are willing to take the time explain to them what they have been trying to learn. I admit that the method is better suited to tutorials or seminars in which there are, say, fewer than 10 students, but it does work in much larger classes, as I know from my own experience.

The way to proceed is not by asking questions willy nilly, simply throwing them out there for students to answer at random. Anyone can do that. And when done ineptly it makes the teacher appear awkward and artificial. Confine your questions to one or two students at a time. Choose another two in the next class, and another two in the next, and so on (as professors do in law school—or at least used to do). This method will intimidate some students, but it works, because attentive students will learn just as much from your questioning of other students as they can from other forms of instruction. A former student of mine confirmed this when he told me that he benefited from listening to me probe and question his classmates as when I probed and questioned him directly because, in both instances, he was going through the same thought process.[6]

Next, you should work from the particular to the general, as discussed above, and as Plato reminds us in Book VI of *The Republic* (which should be closely studied in its entirety). Socratic questioning starts with "hypotheses—that is, steppingstones and springboards—in order to reach what is free from hypotheses at the beginning of the whole." When the student has grasped this, the argument proceeds from this beginning point and "in such fashion goes back down again to an end."[7] Your questions must follow logically so that they build an argument and lead up to some final point, which must be so clear that students grasp it. Otherwise, they will be dazed and confused, and will not have learned, as Aquinas observed. If the structure of your questioning is not evident, it might be necessary to write your questions down or put an outline on the board as you proceed.

Finally, you must fix the impression. Here again repetition is necessary but monotony is deadly. As noted above, good teachers will use a range of examples and associations in various contexts to reinforce key concepts and ideas. They make sure in every class that students have improved, and that each class builds on the lessons of previous classes. They will show the succession of big points over the course as a whole by explaining what students should have learned, filling in the gaps in understanding, pointing out what students have missed, describing outstanding problems that are still to be solved—in short, they will review the ground that has been covered through practice and repetition. There is nothing wrong with letting students know that more work can be done, even as you move on to the next lesson. "One of the worst depressants in school learning," writes Gilbert Highet, "is the feeling that everything is already known and filed away, that knowledge is all dead wood which every generation has to saw up and grind down all over again."

Don't expect students to ask for help. Offer to help them. Begin classes by letting them ask questions on any subject, as professors did in the Middle Ages with *quodlibets* ("whatever you like"), which you can use as a springboard for the lesson of the day. When done properly—that is, clearly, distinctly, orderly, and with great variety—the students' own interest and attention will help them to remember what you are saying. I like to review by asking one student to explain something we discussed in the previous class for the benefit of those who might have missed it or forgotten. I will have him outline the question posed by a reading or the point of class discussion or the issue of a lecture; as he answers, I fill in gaps whenever necessary, correct his mistakes, and support him along the way. The benefit of reviewing in this way is that it forces students to state the central idea clearly and then identify the parts that demonstrate or support it. If they cannot, then it is clear that they haven't grasped the point or learned.

The Socratic method is still the best method of oral instruction, not only because it the most thorough method of instruction, and the most natural and organic way of teaching, but also because it promotes the most genuine form of active learning. It is fostered by daily contact, personal associations and example, conversation, and the sharing of a common life and ambitions. It creates genuine communal learning and feelings of closeness to others, of a loosening of boundaries. In fact, all the features that modern cognitive scientists recognize as essential for active learning—conversation and questioning, feelings of novelty and challenge, a sense of discovery and exploration, a sense of achievement through problem-solving—can be achieved through the Socratic method. As Sandra Johnson writes in *The Neuroscience of Adult Learning*, through "dialogue, the mentor not only attempts to understand the learner's thoughts, but also raises questions that can stimulate the neuronal process of reflection," which is both "*required*" and "a *natural* way of learning."[8]

In Plato's dialogues, Socrates generated active participation among his students, not only because he demonstrated the intrinsic value of education, but also because he knew that the process mattered most. He was never dogmatic or rigid, and therefore turned learning into that "peculiar dynamic state which people experience when they are fully immersed in an activity," what Mihaly Csikszentmihalyi calls *flow*.[9] The Socratic method is the best example of the "wholistic sensation" of total involvement, of doing and being at the same time, that is achieved when teaching is not boring for us, and learning no longer a chore for our students. It raises insights in students and originates in students what they cannot originate themselves. Socrates was a great teacher, writes James P. Carse, because he initiated *thinking* in his students. He exposed the source and then he stepped back. "We know we have met such a teacher when we come away amazed not at what the teacher was thinking but at what we are thinking," he adds. "We forget what the teacher is saying because we are listening to a source deeper than the teachings themselves." This is the appropriate end of liberal education, the ultimate proof that it has succeeded, and why talk about "assessment" and "outcomes" is often misguided in higher education: You can't assess becoming then being. The essence of teaching and learning is in the act themselves, as former football coach Tony Dungy understood very well: "It's the journey that matters. Learning is more important than the test."[10]

Finally, the Socratic method is still the best method of oral instruction because it prevents classroom discussions from lapsing into a no-holds-barred free-for-all, thus serving as a model of what civil discourse should be—not what it typically is in the United States, where people talk past each other because they do not know how to come to terms or listen to each other. Listening means attending to what other people say, as Plutarch writes in a wonderful essay, "On Listening to Lectures," which every teacher and student ought to read.[11] Plutarch points out that listening is not passive behavior naturally acquired, but an extremely complex activity that can be learned and perfected. It takes awareness, concentration, sustained effort, and thought, which most people, including teachers, need to practice. The art of listening means pondering what people say rather than letting it slip through their minds; getting at a speaker's meaning and ferreting out his intentions; even detecting inconsistencies, contradictions, unsubstantiated claims, or attempts to conceal thoughts. Above all, it takes a good-natured disposition, because to listen well means to listen with consideration and good manners. Good listeners, says Plutarch, know how "to sit upright without lounging or sprawling, to look directly at the speaker, to maintain a pose of active attention, and a sedateness of countenance free from any expression, not merely of arrogance or displeasure but even of other thoughts and preoccupations." They avoid rude behavior such as "frowning, a sour face, a roving glance, twisting the body about, smiling, sleepy yams, bowing down the head and all like actions." Good listeners are fully engaged and think of themselves as participants performing with the speaker.

Professors likewise must practice good manners and listen to their students. As an undergraduate I was always put off by professors who interrupted me and my fellow students with contradictions or refutations before we finished speaking. Even worse were those who looked at their notes or were clearly thinking about the next thing they wanted to say while we were talking. It was not only boorish, it was rude; it sent the message that what we said was not important or worthy of serious attention or thought. It also reflected poor planning, clumsiness, perhaps even a lack of knowledge of their subject. Teachers who know their subject will be adept at moving backwards, forwards, even sideways, displaying the mental agility of the expert trial lawyer. If what a student says is out of sequence, there is nothing wrong with acknowledging that or asking her to hold on to that thought because you will return to it later. If wrong, correct the student without barreling her over or making her look or feel foolish. "The authority of those who teach is often an obstacle to those who want to learn," Cicero correctly observed. Students should feel encouraged to speak up in class, ask questions, and give their opinions—although one should never tolerate wrong answers or uniformed views.

Memory is essential for classroom discussions, not only because professors must remember their subject, but also because they must remember what students say. It is crucial to connect your students' comments with the general discussion. Share the stage. Make them look good. Use their points or examples to illustrate your own. Ask them to repeat your questions, or make it appear as if they came up with the ideas you planned to talk about. Return to points from the current discussion or from previous classes. Ask questions like, "Remember two weeks ago when you brought up that point? Have you changed your mind now? Do you still see it in the same way?" Reinforce points that other students have made by asking the one being questioned if she agrees or disagrees. These kinds of connections engage students in the discourse and reinforce knowledge by building on previous lessons. But it means thinking through things yourself, anticipating objections or questions or issues that students might have. Professors who learn something to teach it will have difficulty doing this; professors who teach what they know are more likely to reflect on the subject, think about its problems, raise new questions, and so on. Plutarch suggests two ways to encourage the habit of attentive listening: one is to insist that listeners ask questions themselves; another is to "propose some problem which is useful and essential."

Scholars of teaching and learning like Stephen D. Brookfield and Stephen Preskill, authors of *Discussion as a Way of Teaching*, add little to what Plutarch has already said, but they are taken seriously because they are "up-to-date" and their approach is modern and scientific, not based on anecdote or tradition. They have identified specific problems, developed methods to solve them, applied those methods, studied the feedback or results, and measured the outcomes. Above all else, they supply teachers with a nifty formula to follow: (1) begin every lecture with one or more questions that you're trying to answer; (2) end every lecture with a series of questions that have been raised or unanswered; (3) introduce periods of silence for thought and reflection; (4) deliberately introducing alternative perspectives; (5) introduce periods of assumptive hunting; (6) use buzz groups.[12]

To be sure, Plutarch wasn't advanced enough to think of buzz groups, which consist of three or four students who once or twice during a lecture discuss an issue that arises and consider such questions as these:

- What's the most contentious statement you've heard so far in the lecture today?

- What's the most important point that's been made in the lecture so far?
- What question would you most like to have answered regarding the topic of the lecture today?
- What's the most unsupported assertion you've heard in the lecture so far?
- Of all the ideas and point you've heard so far, which is most obscuring or ambiguous to you?

But is it always necessary to write down each question and answer it formally? Why not encourage students to ask and answer these questions mentally, or address them orally during the course of a lecture or a discussion, as an artist would do? That would exercise memory and encourage the art of listening—developing habits of thought and mind like awareness, concentration, sustained effort—what Wayne C. Booth calls "Listening-Rhetoric," or the "whole range of communicative arts for reducing misunderstanding by paying full attention to opposing views." The pleasure of listening, says Plutarch, is not an end in itself; it is a useful tool that can change us, an art that promotes independent thinking and right living. It is, reiterates Lord Chesterfield, the mark of a civilized human being. What Brookfield and Preskill illustrate yet again is the tendency among modern scholars of teaching and learning to mechanize methods and reduce teaching to steps that need only be followed to make teachers effective. Like the dean at the liberal arts college where I taught, they make teaching and learning seem artificial, stilted, and stiff.

One way to avoid this kind of artificiality is to make your points or arguments *appear* as if they have arisen naturally from the discussion. This approach is effective because it is informal, fluid, and natural. If done well, students won't realize that these "lecturettes" have been planned in advance, and they are therefore likely to be more attentive because what you say seems spontaneous—whereas the opposite happens if they feel they are being lectured at ("Today I am going to address … " and eyes start glazing over). "Most observations please better when they appear to be conceived on the moment" and "spring from the subject itself as we discuss it," Quintilian teaches. It's a matter of timing, finding the right place to insert what you have planned to tell them all along. It's also important to explain what you are doing as you are doing it—which is chiefly what distinguishes teaching from general public speaking. Ask questions aloud, as if asking yourself, such as: What additional sources should be consulted? What other problems or questions arise? You will show them that your subject is a process of thinking and you will reinforce what you are discussing because your lecture will be *a part of* the discussion. But if you lay down your course of proof beforehand, you cut off all pleasure of novelty and discovery.

This is the chief reason and why online education can never replace traditional liberal education, and why online courses are insufficient for undergraduate instruction, even though they are here to stay. A recent study suggests that most college students will be taking classes online by the year 2014, and the Obama administration is doing its part to accelerate this trend. A 2009 article in *The Christian Science Monitor* reported that the Department of Education "plans to create free, online courses for the nation's 1,200 community colleges—which teach nearly half of undergrads—to make it easier for students to learn basic skills for jobs. The courses would be offered as part of a 'national skills college' managed by the department." The President himself provided the rationale. The way "to build a firmer, stronger foundation" for economic growth, he wrote in the *Washington Post*, is "to create the jobs of the future within our borders" and to "give our workers the skills and training they need to compete for those jobs." Community colleges will spearhead the charge and "serve as 21st-century job training centers, working with local businesses to help workers learn the skills they need to fill the jobs of the future."[13]

Not surprisingly, many students like the idea. Online education gives them flexibility, not only to learn at their own pace, but to accommodate their busy lives. As one student who is working toward his master's of science degree said on NPR's *Talk of the Nation*, he preferred taking his courses online because traditional universities require him to go a main campus for classes. "And I just—I can't do that. I've got kids, and I've got a wife. It's just not a choice." Another caller, a student of midwifery in Boulder, Colorado, affirmed that online education serves a useful purpose in helping students like her to get the degrees and the skills they need to be more competitive workers: "I have a very busy midwifery practice of children, and now I am able to go ahead and finish my program in a rigorous program that, It's offering me an excellent education [sic]." But perhaps the real reason students like online education, suggests Kevin Carey, policy director of Education Sector, is that it offers a viable and affordable alternative to brick-and-mortar colleges and universities, especially as the cost of tuition keeps skyrocketing and students incur unprecedented levels of debt.[14]

I am not opposed to online education. In principle, it is a laudable endeavor because it attempts to make higher education accessible to greater numbers of people—and I am in favor of any medium that encourages curiosity and helps students to learn. As mentioned above, I use the Internet in all my classes and have web sites for each course. I have taught hybrid courses and found Moodle. Blackboard, and Angel to be effective and have integrated them successfully into my teaching. I have also used such web sites as BookGlutton.com, which has transformed the way my students read and discuss certain texts.

I also don't oppose online education because many online classes are merely money-makers, cash cows as the saying goes, much like M.B.A. and master's degree in education programs that many smaller colleges have built up to improve their cash flow. Nor do I oppose online instruction because it reinforces the notion that higher education is a means to accumulate gobs of information and obtain a degree. Colleges and universities have been doing both long before the Internet was invented. The issue isn't technology, or even online education itself, but whether online courses can help students achieve the aims of liberal education better than traditional modes of instruction, such as rigorous classroom discussion. To date there is no evidence to support the assertion, although proponents of online education claim that it can.

One reason, according to Linda F. Cornelious and Yi Yang, is that online courses promote student collaboration which develops "personal understanding of content."[15] But other studies suggest the opposite, maintaining that for collaboration to be effective it must be face-to-face. In instances where groups are mixed by race, interaction reduces racial prejudice, and may even prevent attrition among minority students and help them integrate into academic life.[16]

There is much additional evidence to suggest that people not only "require positive social interaction and nurturance in order to learn," but also "probably engage more effectively in brain-altering learning when they are face-to-face, mind-to-mind, and heart-to-heart." That's because the brain "flourishes best within the context of social interaction." In fact, through such human signs as "emotional facial expressions, physical contact, and eye gaze—even through pupil dilation and blushing—people are in constant, if often unconscious, two-way communication with those around them." Learning is more meaningful, and "brains are sculpted, balanced, and made healthy," in personal learning environments.[17]

Similarly, both John T. Cacioppo, a neuroscientist with the University of Chicago, and Michael J. Bugeja, a professor of communications at Iowa State University, have suggested that modern digital technology gives people a false sense of connection, and that it may even increase feelings of isolation and loneliness. Not only has that the Internet failed to create a closer global community, as promised, writes Bugeja, it has succeeded in producing an "interpersonal divide" when people spend more time in virtual communities than they do interacting in the real world.[18] Even the 2010 Education Department report, which is pro-online instruction, acknowledges that, despite "what appears to be strong support for online learning applications, the studies in this meta-analysis *do not demonstrate that online learning is superior as a medium*;" at best, "when used by itself, online learning *appears* to offer a *modest advantage* over conventional classroom instruction" (italics added). That might sound encouraging, but not when measured against current student outcomes.[19]

Another reason online instruction is purportedly superior to traditional modes is that it promotes "nondiscriminatory teaching and learning practices since the teachers and students, as well as students and their classmates typically don't meet face-to-face." Since "students cannot tell the race, gender, physical characteristics of each other and their teachers," say Cornelious and Yang, "online education presents a bias-free teaching and learning environment for instructors and students." But is this what education—let alone *higher* education—should be about? Should we keep our students from having to explain who they are and to justify what they believe to others in real-life settings? Should we be shielding them from the kinds of confrontations that they will face in the great world because they get uncomfortable? Do we really want to replace the face-to-face experiences that are essential for undergraduate education to thrive with virtual encounters—much like Facebook and MySpace substitute real interaction and genuine relationships with other human beings with virtual "friends?" Online courses highlight the tendency in education at all levels in the United States today, not only to sanitize the educational experience for students, but to sanitize life.

At its best, liberal education creates personal contact and friendships between students themselves and their teachers, and it provides them with encounters that increase their knowledge, develop their skills, refine their tastes, and expose them to the unfamiliar. But at big schools and small, the trend—whether hiring more adjunct instructors to teach lower-level courses or discouraging faculty from devoting time to their students by forcing them to obsess over research and publications—is to push teachers and students further away from each other and those experiences. I am not blaming online education; it is not the problem. Rather, online education is merely a symptom of a larger trend in higher education and another indication that liberal education has been devalued as a whole. Not only is the kind of personal contact and engagement that students get from such activities as classroom discussions at the heart of liberal education, it is precisely what undergraduate students need and want.

According to the Center of Inquiry in the Liberal Arts at Wabash College, a vast majority said that their education was more meaningful to them when these contacts existed, especially with professors who were not distant figures or only remotely accessible. Among the study's criteria for good teaching were a high quality of interaction with students; the interest that faculty showed in teaching and student development; the extent to which faculty were genuinely interested in teaching; prompt feedback; and the quality of nonclassroom interactions between students and faculty. But a majority of students reported that they experienced these practices and conditions only "sometimes" or "occasionally." At small institutions, only 44% said these were strong, as compared with a meager 28% at larger institutions. In fact, many have used such statistics to prove their point about the superiority of online education. As the student of midwifery said, "I have a whole lot of interaction with my professors, far more so, actually, than I had when I had the walls and roof over me."

That may be true for this student, just as it is for students who feel satisfied in traditional brick-and-mortar institutions, but it is also true that online courses are more likely to reinforce the kind of adolescent behavior that distracts undergraduates from developing intellectual maturity and the habits of thought and mind appropriate to the liberally educated person. The reality that proponents of online education ignore is that it is easier for students to shut off or block out opinions or views that might unsettle them run or contrary to their own while they are hiding behind computer screens. They are more likely to "multitask" while online—check e-mail, chat with friends, view other web sites, Tweet, listen to music, talk on mobile phones, or even watch TV—when they should be attending to the issue at hand, and actually learn less in the process.[20] As UCLA psychology professor Russell Poldrak discovered, "multitasking adversely affects how you learn. Even if you learn while multitasking, that learning is less flexible and more specialized, so you cannot retrieve the information as easily." Like traditional lectures, online instruction succeeds only with students who are mature and motivated to learn and capable of seeing the Internet and the World Wide Web as tools, not as ends in themselves.

But that's clearly not the case. Students already have access to great books, complete libraries, masterpieces of art, and classical music online, but for the overwhelming majority technology is used and valued for entertainment and social networking.[21] All the information available at their fingertips is worthless if they lack judgment and the ability to use it appropriately. And there is no evidence that online instruction will change students' behavior. Our inability to control the learning environment makes it almost certain that they will not achieve the full educational experience that activities like classroom discussions provide, or that they will not learn what we are trying to teach them beyond accumulating information to pass a course and get a degree. Our job as educators is not to keep students in "mental swaddling clothes," as Harold Laski writes, but to remove ignorance, impart knowledge, and develop intelligence—in a word, promote intellectual maturity.

The real issue is that modern educators are failing to give students an educational experience that they cannot get anywhere else, including online. Colleges and universities, thinking they are too important and too big to fail, have become, like General Motors, oversized, overvalued, and are peddling products that most people need but few people want. But when students are told that they must have a college degree to succeed in today's world, can we blame them if they seek more online courses because they are cheaper and make it easier for them to get credentialed? We may very well end up with more people with degrees in this country than anywhere else in the world by 2020, as President Obama's plan calls for. But who is asking, "What kinds of citizens will they be?"

CHAPTER 5

WHY GREAT BOOKS STILL MATTER

Many a man lives a burden to the earth; but a good book is the precious life-blood of a master spirit, embalmed and treasured up on purpose to a life beyond life.

~ Milton, *Aeropagitica*

It might surprise you that only a little more than one third of Americans can name the three branches of government. Only name them. Not identify their functions or explain why there are three branches instead of two or only one. It surprised me when I heard former Supreme Court Justice Sandra Day O'Connor state that statistic on The Daily Show with Jon Stewart.[1] A few days later I was giving a quiz and decided to offer students some "extra credit" if they answered additional questions, the first of which was: "Name the three branches of government." About half of them got the answer right, and many of my students had just taken a civics exam less than a year before to graduate from high school.

Perhaps if students and Americans in general read more they might know these things. But in 2005, 65% of college freshmen said they read little or nothing for pleasure, and in 2006, one in four Americans didn't read a single book.[2] And those who did, for the most part, were not reading difficult or challenging books, but *Marley & Me* by John Grogan, *Culture Warrior* by Bill O'Reilly, and *The Da Vinci Code* by Dan Brown. The most

---

The Skinny on Teaching: What You Don't Learn in Graduate School, pp. 59–72
Copyright © 2011 by Information Age Publishing
All rights of reproduction in any form reserved.

popular subjects were, and still are, mysteries, thrillers, and romance. Americans want to be entertained, and if reading is not like watching TV, they get bored. "I just get sleepy when I read," said Richard Bustos of Dallas who would rather spend time in his backyard pool than reading (not even reading a book by his pool). At the time of the interview, he was in his 30s and a college graduate but had not read a single book in 2006. As a project manager for a telecommunications company, he apparently has no intellectual advantage from his education over people who never went to college, probably many of those he supervises. Clearly his "higher" education has failed because it could not cultivate the habit of reading, never mind the reading of serious or challenging books.

If you asked Bustos, and most other Americans for that matter, I suppose they would say that they can read. In one sense, they are probably right, if they mean the activity that takes place when the mind operates independently on the symbols of readable matter. But reading in the sense that I mean is more than the deciphering of symbols from various printed media; it is an intellectual activity that occurs on different levels and requires concentration, sustained effort, discrimination, and judgment. It is also an essential part of undergraduate education because it is a form of instruction, and because it promotes the act of discovery. As instruction it furnishes the mind with knowledge of something through the written word; as discovery it is necessary for research, investigation, or reflection (or some combination of these). In either case, writes Mortimer Adler in his now classic work, *How to Read a Book*, the mind is elevated "by the power of its own operations" and "passes from understanding less to understanding more."[3] Reading in this sense is no more passive than learning because readers are engaged and they strive to overcome the state of inequality that exists between their minds and the minds of authors. Reading, in this sense, *is* learning because it is inseparable from thinking.

"To read well, that is, to read true books in a true spirit," writes Thoreau, "is a noble exercise, and one that will task the reader more than any exercise which the customs of the day esteem. It requires training such as the athletes underwent, the steady intention almost of the whole life to this object." The best way to turn undergraduate students into what Thoreau calls "alert and heroic readers" is through the great books, the masterpieces of the civilized tradition, which must be central to the entire undergraduate curriculum. The great books are essential to liberal education because (1) they connect students with the past; (2) they educate students as they read them; (3) they reinforce the varieties of knowledge, the skills, and the habits of thought and mind appropriate to free and cultured human beings; and (4) they teach students how to read. Simply put, the great books must be central to the undergraduate curriculum because they are the best and most efficient means to achieve all four of these aims simultaneously and foster genuine *synergy of learning*.

A great book can be any book in which one keeps finding something new. It seems inexhaustible as a source of knowledge or wisdom and therefore one does not tire of reading it. A great book is thick, not necessarily in size, but in the density of its content, ideas, and subject matter, as in Karl Marx's *Communist Manifesto*, John Stuart Mill's *On Liberty*, or Joseph Conrad's *Heart of Darkness*. A great book is adaptable because the knowledge one extracts from it transcends place and time, despite its having been written in a particular historical context, such as Homer's *Iliad*, Shakespeare's *Plays*, and *The Federalist Papers*. There may be no universal or permanent canon of great books, any more than there are universal or permanent viewpoints among the authors of great books themselves, but there are books that most educated people would agree are great, even if they have never read them, as Mark Twain once said.[4] Although the definition of a great book may ultimately be subjective, much like the definition of an American, intelligent readers will be able to state and discuss their reasons for what makes a great book.

What it comes down to is that a book is worth re-reading because it says something personally useful and meaningful, as Machiavelli describes in his famous letter to Francesco Vettori:

> When evening has come, I return to my house and go into my study. At the door, I take off my clothes of the day, covered with mud and mire, and I put on my regal and courtly garments; and decently reclothed, I enter the ancient courts of ancient men, where, received by them lovingly, I feed on the food that alone is mine and that I was born for. There I am not ashamed to speak with them and to ask them the reason for their actions; and they in their humanity reply to me. And for the space of four hours I feel no boredom, I forget every pain, I do not fear poverty, death does not frighten me. I deliver myself entirely to them.[5]

The classics of antiquity created a society for Machiavelli that would otherwise have been unavailable to him during his exile to his villa outside Florence. Montaigne read great books in the solitude of his chateau and treated them as if they were written by his contemporaries: "Whatever language my books speak, I speak to them in my own." For Tocqueville the authors of great books were companions as he traveled across America: "There are three men with whom I live a little every day," he wrote to his friend Louis de Kergorlay; "they are Pascal, Montesquieu, and Rousseau." Even Socrates learned from great minds through their books, Xenophon tells us, which became a source for his friendships:

> "Antiphon," said Socrates, "as another man gets pleasure from a good horse, or a dog, or a bird, I get even more pleasure from good friends. And if I have something good, I teach it to them with respect to virtue. And together with my friends I go through the treasures of the wise men of old which they left

behind written in books, and peruse them. If we see something good, we pick it out and hold it to be a great profit, if we are able to prove useful to one another."

"When I heard this," wrote Xenophon, "I held Socrates to be really happy."[6]

The great books connect students with the past because they invite them to listen to and participate in the great conversations of the ages. "Great books of every civilization," says Thoreau, "are the voices of human experience and as such worth reading and pondering." They are a form of travel in time and space, allowing our students to experience vicariously what others have thought, felt, and even seen. They enlarge students' perspectives and strip them of their provincialism. They can free them from their self-imposed nonage and transform them, as Candide was transformed in Voltaire's story, a modern version of Plato's Allegory of the Cave.

Candide believed that he lived in the best of all possible worlds, that Westphalia was the best of all places, Thunder-ten-tronck the best of all castles, Pangloss the wisest of all men, and Cunégonde the most beautiful of all women ... until he was caught kissing her and kicked out of the province. Then his real education began. He discovered that people in other parts of the world lived and acted and thought differently than the people in Thunder-ten-tronck. In Peru, he encountered two women whose lovers were monkeys and saw firsthand that people could have different customs and standards of morality. In Eldorado, a place "unknown to the rest of the world, and where all nature is of a sort so different from ours," he compared the natives' way of living with those of Europeans and admitted for the first time in his life, against everything he had been told, "that all was pretty bad in Westphalia." Candide's conclusion: "travel is certainly necessary."

Voltaire teaches us through Candide, who left the cave of Westphalia, how to leave the caves of our own lives and overcome the Idols of our Minds. Only the author of a great book, observed Thoreau, "speaks to the intellect and health of mankind, to all in any age who can understand him." Read and taught properly, the great books can have the same effect on our students because they expose them to the vast store of experience accumulated over the ages and transform them into thoughtful and reflective human beings; they teach them questions that are essential for living a good life, as well as viable answers to those questions; they compel them to consider fundamental alternatives to the problems they face today, even liberate them from historical necessity and a dependence on custom and tradition; above all, they open up new pathways of thought and press them to test the validity and cogency of their assumptions.

"If books are to be liberating," writes Allan Bloom in his Foreword to *Emile*, "they must seem implausible in the half-light of our plausibilities which we no longer know how to question."[7] An old book must appear to be old-fashioned, he adds, and readers must try to see the questions as their authors saw them, get inside their books, and observe the world through unfamiliar eyes. They should not simply think of the authors as the products of their times, but as shaping their times. "It is an unending task," Bloom says elsewhere, "one that continually evokes that wonder at what previously seemed a commonplace which Aristotle says is the origin of philosophy." Once we show our students how to make this effort they will begin to see themselves and society with the detachment that is necessary for proper examination. Along the way they learn something about the past, but more importantly, they will learn something about themselves. They may still be ignorant about many things, like Candide, but they will be wiser than before. Reading is certainly necessary.

The proof of a great book is in the reading. Eventually students will determine for themselves the merits of one book over another and supply reasons for their choices, but they have to start somewhere. Having been trained for the pursuit of a lifetime, they will return to some authors, discard others, find new ones along the way. Once initiated, they are likely to agree with Thoreau that "later writers, say what we will of their genius, have rarely, if ever, equalled the elaborate beauty and finish and the lifelong and heroic literary labors of the ancients. They only talk of forgetting them who never knew them. It will be soon enough to forget them when we have the learning and the genius which will enable us to attend to and appreciate them."

Lincoln, an autodidactic who read the Bible, Euclid's *Elements*, and Shakespeare's *Plays* as deliberately and thoughtfully as they were written, understood what Thoreau meant; so did William Dean Howells, who describes in his autobiography the passion for reading among his fellow townsmen in Ohio in the 1840s. These men not only represent an age that believed in the great books as a natural source of knowledge about the world and the place to go to satisfy curiosity about life; they remind us that most great books were written for ordinary intelligent readers, not a handful of specialists, who often give the impression that it is more necessary to read what they say about the great books to understand them than it is to read the great books themselves, deadening wonder and the thrill of discovery they offer.

The great books educate students by providing them with shared knowledge and experiences that are necessary for a pluralistic society like ours; they encourage dialogue and discussion through mutual confidence and good will; they promote communication through embedded references and a common vocabulary which will enable them to understand each other. How many readers grasped my meaning as soon as I mentioned *Candide* because they have read the book themselves? How many—even among college and university graduates—will have missed the point?

"Education will be saved," writes Mark Van Doren, "only when it is agreed that men must know the same things—which does not mean that they will believe the same things."[8] Although many colleges and universities attempt to provide a shared intellectual experience through so-called Foundations courses or Cultural Heritage or Liberal Studies, they fail, quite frankly, because they are peripheral to the curriculum, not taken seriously by faculty, and viewed by most students as an intrusion on their education as vocational training.

The great books must be central to the entire undergraduate curriculum, even the physical sciences, because they are both broad enough to show the boundaries of various subjects, and focused enough for students to realize the intellectual depth of each. They allow students to wrestle with the essentials of any field directly while disciplining the mind, illuminating it, and teaching it how to reduce facts to order; as tools of instruction, they combine both the particular information and the general knowledge with which liberal education aims to furnish the mind. Studying "with the proper care the great books which the greatest minds have left behind," writes Harold Laski, is the essence of liberal education—"a study in which the more experienced pupils assist the less experienced pupils, including the beginners."

I am not suggesting that only the great books must be read and taught, as at St. John's College, or that everything else be excluded from the undergraduate curriculum, including majors. I've used Richard Tarnas's *The Passion of the Western Mind* as a main text for Western Civilization courses, and Diarmaid MacCulloch's *The Reformation* for an upper-level and graduate course on Reformation Europe. I know American historians who use Howard Zinn's *People's History of the United States*, a psychologist who has used Steven Pinker's *How the Mind Works,* and an English professor who has used such books as *Mountains Beyond Mountains* and *Newjack* to expose students to new ideas and new ways to read. However, neither these nor any other good book that could be used as a main text for a course should replace the great books, which must be central to the entire undergraduate curriculum because they promote genuine *synergy of learning*, as I demonstrated earlier with my Bacon and Descartes example, and shall discuss further in the next chapter.

That means getting rid of pre-packaged textbooks, the kind peddled by the major publishers, now replete with color pictures and CDs and corresponding web sites—literally, bells and whistles. Textbooks are dull, they are always expensive, and they give the impression that knowledge can be packaged into neat little compartments.[9] Students need books that are engaging, critical, skeptical, and challenging—which textbooks can never be; and they must see books as interesting and important for their own sake—which textbooks can never foster. They are "toneless teachers," as

Mark Van Doren called them, which students treat as fountains of information that must be remembered to get a good grade. Nowadays publishers even supply teachers with lecture materials, PowerPoints, and test materials, which probably explains why a majority of college students are taking multiple-choice exams.[10]

Both textbooks and multiple-choice exams are a scourge to higher education. Just as multiple-choice exams do little to promote critical thinking, pre-packaged textbooks do little to cultivate the habit of reading that we want our students to take away from the college experience. When I have assigned a pre-packaged text, most of my students tell me that they stop reading it at some point during the semester; at the end, they sell it back to the bookstore, which shows just how little they value it. For Harold Laski, the final test of a college or university, was not only whether it created a widespread curiosity in books, but also whether it awakened students to the study of great books. Why should students be denied access to the greatest minds? Why should they learn about things rather than gain knowledge of things? "The second-handedness of the learned," says A. N. Whitehead, "is the secret of its mediocrity."

Putting the great books at the center of the undergraduate curriculum also means teaching them in their entirety. Reading excerpted passages here and there will not promote personal exploration or get students into the habit of reading entire books. The practice is convenient—I do it myself—but admittedly harmful if we are trying to teach students to think their own thoughts. In the first place, professors do the work for students by taking away their responsibility to find the important or relevant or significant passages. They also remove students' ability to see the work as a whole. Who would teach art history by showing *only* details of various paintings by Michelangelo, Bernini, or David rather than entire works of their art? Or music by having students *only* listen to clips from Bach, Beethoven, and Brahms rather than entire concertos or symphonies? Or a play by Shakespeare, Ibsen, or Beckett by watching *only* one scene rather than the whole play? "They that only study abridgements," writes Bacon, "like men who would visit all places, pass through every place in such post as they have no time to observe as they go or make profit of their travel."[11]

In the second place, excerpts inhibit the imaginative understanding and the possibility of transforming students' minds, as happened in the class in which I assigned Flaubert's *Madame Bovary*. Before reading the book, every student said that adultery is absolutely wrong and inexcusable; after reading it, many students had changed their minds. They still believed that adultery was wrong, but they exonerated Emma because Flaubert had masterfully recreated the longings of passion in her soul and the oppressive bourgeois world that drove her to commit her sin. Their imaginative understanding would never have been stirred had they read a chapter here and a chapter there.

No doubt even good books can do this, but the additional advantage to reading a great book like *Madame Bovary* is that it is the best and most efficient means to achieve the ends of liberal education simultaneously, as I'll also show in the next chapter. As a primary source it is universal, not in the sense that it explains everything, but in the sense that it gives students a complete vision of Flaubert's world as he saw it at the time. When studied with other great books, such as Stendhal's *The Red and the Black* and Zola's *Germinal*, it educates students as they read it because it teaches them about the tradition of literature within which Flaubert is writing, it helps them to establish appropriate connections, and it introduces new patterns of thought that are essential for learning and memory to form, as I discussed earlier.

The value of reading books in this way, modern cognitive science informs us, is that past learning "*always* influences the acquisition of new learning."[12] In fact, the "more connections that students can make between past learning and new learning, the more likely they are to determine sense and meaning and thus retain the new learning," writes David A. Sousa. And "when these connections can be extended across curriculum areas," he adds, "they establish a framework of associative networks that will be recalled for future problem solving." Not only does this reinforce what William James said about the nature of learning, it highlights the chief defect in higher education today and an important reason why students are not learning to think critically.

This leads to the third reason the great books are useful, and that's because they reinforce the varieties of knowledge, the skills, and the habits of thought and mind appropriate to the free and cultured human being. The great books are the most practical texts that students can read precisely because they are the most intellectually challenging books they can read. They expose students to momentous ideas while teaching them how to penetrate to the root of things, follow their intellect, and acquire genuine understanding. They force students to stretch their minds by thinking through complex arguments in all fields of inquiry. They never enforce conformity of thought, they are never monolithic, they never indoctrinate. Those who read them to confirm what they believe, says Harvey Mansfield, do not really read them.

The great books teach students to read, the fourth reason they are useful, not for paltry convenience, but in "a high sense," as Thoreau writes, as "a noble intellectual exercise" during which "we have to stand on tip-toe to read and devote our most alert and wakeful hours to." This is why "going to college and taking hard classes changes the brain more than taking easy classes," writes cognitive scientist Eric Jensen. The "human brain is designed to interact with the world and makes changes, depending on the quality of interaction." Positive and sustained interactions produce one set of changes, while negative and intense interactions produce another set. "We change based on our life experiences," which includes our educational experiences.[13] It is precisely because the great books are difficult and require a high level of mental exertion that they are the best instruments for shaping the habits of thought and mind in our students.

Finally, putting the great books at the center of the undergraduate curriculum also means having them taught by professors from all departments and fields. Let the mathematician teach Plato; the philosopher teach Bach; the musician teach Shakespeare; the professor of literature teach Adam Smith; the economist teach Hegel; the historian teach Euclid or Newton. If we are going to require students to study the great books, professors ought to be required to demonstrate their ability to teach them as well. They should also be able to show how they have integrated them into their own work and lives, and this includes science and mathematics, as Morris Kline has pointed out: "I believe as firmly as I have in the past that a mathematics course addressed to liberal arts students must present the scientific and humanistic import of the subject … . In fact, the branches of elementary mathematics were created primarily to serve extra-mathematical needs and interests. In the very act of meeting such needs each of these creations has proved to have inestimable importance for man's understating of the nature of his world and himself."[14] Not only future scientists and mathematicians need a solid foundation in the principles of science and mathematics; future citizens must possess a fundamental understating of how science and mathematics work. The classic texts from these subjects promote the aims of liberal education as much as those from history, literature, philosophy, and the other humanities.

For most students, undergraduate education is the only time they will have in their lives to understand their fundamental assumptions, challenge their premises, examine their beliefs, and consider viable alternatives.[15] By training them to become alert and heroic readers, the great books promote self-examination because they force them to slow down and reflect, to look for role models, to observe themselves and the world around them in a new light. They give students time to discover a sense of plot and character, an eye for structure and arguments, an ear for style. They cultivate taste and judgment and an esthetic vision by exposing them to fine things. In short, they promote intellectual maturity and develop cognitive abilities, rather than simply inundate them with facts and stuff their heads with data. In fact, exposure to too much information can actually be dangerous to students and interfere with understanding because it "comes too fast for [them] to integrate and comprehend," writes cognitive scientist James Zull. The implication for teaching and learning is worse, he adds, because there is "constant pressure to increase the amount of information in our classes." Our students are living in an "information age," not an "understanding age," and modern-day colleges and universities are contributing to this trend when they should be resisting it.[16]

Modern studies also confirm that the more students read books in relation to each other, the more they can read, since genuine learning takes place through appropriate connections and associations, as I discussed earlier, and cognitive scientist Eric Jensen affirms: The evidence is clear "that the more you learn, the more you *can* learn. Complex, environmental enhancement produces higher levels of proteins associated with learning and memory."[17] That's because complexity challenges the brain better than anything else and fosters genuine *synergy of learning*. But now that the great books have been removed from the center of the curriculum in most colleges and universities, and no satisfactory alternative has been found, the educational experience of college students has been seriously diminished, as the authors of *Academically Adrift* have shown.

It's not simply that student outcomes are poor. I'll admit, if I had been tested as a senior on what I learned in biology my freshman year, or in economics my sophomore year, I probably would have failed; but if one compared my disposition, mindset, and intellectual outlook, as a senior, to what they were as a freshman, one would have seen an entirely different person. That's the real failing of colleges and universities today. They are not turning students into mature, thinking beings with appropriate dispositions. Instead, students graduate ignorant of tradition and the knowledge that has been learned and accumulated over time. They leave college or university ignorant of the reasons for the values they embrace, such as toleration, human rights, and freedom of speech. They believe these values are important but do not know why they are important, why they developed, why they might be different or the same, and in what respects. If pressed, they certainly couldn't explain why. They possess not knowledge but assumptions, dogmas, or opinions at best.

Almost 70 years ago, in a speech before the Association for the Advancement of Science (December 1940), Walter Lippmann warned us this was coming:

> The thesis I venture to submit to you is as follows: That during the past forty or fifty years those who are responsible for education have progressively removed from the curriculum of studies the Western culture which produced the modern democratic state; That the schools and colleges have, therefore, been sending out into the world men who no longer understand the creative principle of the society in which they must live; That deprived of their cultural tradition, the newly educated Western men no longer possess in the form and substance of their own minds and spirits and ideas, the premises,

the rationale, the logic, the method, the values of the deposited wisdom which are the genius of the development of Western civilization; That the prevailing education is destined, if it continues, to destroy Western civilization and is in fact destroying it.

George Bernard Shaw, certainly no reactionary, echoed Lippmann's warning and cautioned us against ignoring our tradition. One of the "main objects of education," he writes, "is to prevent people from defeating their own civilization by refusing to tolerate novelties and heresies which history proves they had better tolerate." Not surprisingly, modern cognitive scientists substantiate what Shaw says. Acquired learning goes beyond individuals toward the transmission of culture from generation to generation. In this sense, tradition is like memory in that it is a means for "behavioral adaptation" and a "powerful force for social progress." The loss of memory, like the loss of tradition, "leads to loss of contact with one's immediate self, with one's life history, and with other human beings."[18] This is precisely where we are headed if higher education continues perpetuating intellectual nonage. Tradition is not indoctrination but where past meets present. It is, writes Mark Van Doren, "the medium through which we understand one another when communication takes place. It is the only way of knowing what we are.... It is what leaves novelty possible, in science or in art, for it marks the end from which beginnings can be made. Without it there can be no progress of any sort, and civilization dies."

Consider the "Western" tradition, which has been under assault in academe over the past 40 years. Simply because there is a "Western" tradition does not mean that its great books are Eurocentric, provincial, or exclusive. If anything, the opposite is true. Historically, the outreach of the "West" has been greater than that of other civilizations; the "West" has taken an interest in people, societies, cultures from other parts of the globe; and "Westerners" have learned their languages, translated their literature, disseminated their ideas. Socrates considered himself a citizen of the world, not just of Athens. The ancient Romans were imperialistic by today's standards, but they were certainly no more imperialistic than the Arabs who conquered and occupied North Africa in the eighth century, or the Japanese who invaded China in the twentieth century; they were simply more successful at obtaining and maintaining the territories they conquered. The British colonized India for more than 200 years and imposed "Western" values on Indians, but these included such ideas as common law and human rights, which ultimately undermined British imperial rule and are an integral part of Indian society today. They also opened up the great Indian heritage to Europeans and Americans, including Transcendentalists like Thoreau, who in turn argued that that the great books *of every civilization* must be read.

What critics of the "Western" tradition really want is to eliminate the perceived hegemony of Western values and replace them with a perceived diversity of values from Asia, Africa, or South America, which they believe promote inclusion and toleration and understanding in an age of globalization. So they appeal to our prejudices and try to make us feel guilty for upholding the importance and value of the great books of the West by maligning their authors as racist or sexist or elitist. Who? Montaigne, Suarez, and Voltaire, who exposed and condemned European hypocrisy toward natives in the New World? Mary Wollstonecraft and John Stuart Mill, who argued for the rights of women? Rousseau, Marx, and Whitman, who sided with the common man? Are there elements of racism, sexism, and elitism in some great books of the West? Yes. Are their elements of racism, sexism, and elitism in non-Western great books and contemporary writings for that matter? Yes. Should we not read these books either for the same reason? The great books *of every civilization* are as flawed and as perfect as can be because they are written by human beings about the human condition. But they have also been written by some of the most radical thinkers on record. If read and studied properly, they will genuinely open students' minds *and* impart knowledge, remove ignorance, and develop their intelligence.

Frederick Douglas and W. E. B. DuBois found this out firsthand. Douglas, while still a slave, realized that literature could liberate and he "set out with high hope, and fixed purpose, at whatever cost of trouble, to learn how to read;" and DuBois, writing in 1902, under the oppression of Jim Crow, describes how he sat "with Shakespeare and he winces not. Across the color line I move arm in arm with Balzac and Dumas, where smiling men and welcoming women glide in gilded halls. From out of the caves of Evening that swing between the strong-limbed earth and the tracery of the stars, I summon Aristotle and Aurelius and what soul I will, and they come all graciously with no scorn nor condescension."[19]

So did Edmund Shorris's students in the Clemente Course at Bard College, which I mentioned earlier. They studied moral philosophy though such classics as Plato's *Apology of Socrates* and Aristotle's *Nicomachean Ethics*; and they were introduced to the tradition of American political thought through Magna Carta, Locke's *Two Treatises of Government*, the Declaration of Independence, and documents of the Revolution and the Civil War. After taking his class, one woman who had been fired from her job had become emboldened to start a union; another man, who had a history of violent behavior and who found himself in a situation that could have sent him back to jail, asked himself, "What would Socrates do?" This woman and this man found intellectual liberation through the great books precisely because they understood "the radical character of the humanities," as Shorris puts it.

So have some of my own students. I have been placing the great books at the center of my courses ever since I began teaching at the community college, and invariably students find some way to connect with them. One student, who was the first in his family to attend college and eventually became a police officer, wrote in an e-mail to the chair of my department that "never before, in all my years of school, have I ever experienced a class like this. I couldn't believe I was actually enjoying a History class. For the first time in my life I WANTED to learn. I WANTED to read the text, and I WANTED more of it.... Sure, any professor could have stood up in front of the classroom, and instructed us to read this book or write that paper, but this man did everything with a passion, enthusiasm, and in a fun way like no other professor I have seen before. And like I said, the result is a student that wants to read, and wants to think for myself."

At the state university where I taught, another student, who was born in Jamaica and moved to Brooklyn in his teens, asked me for a list of additional books that he could read on his own after the semester (please excuse his awkward writing): "I am honestly interested in furthering my knowledge in whichever direction these books that you plan to suggest to me will take me. I have enjoyed Machiavelli and Luther and other readings you have suggested. Even though many have probably told you this your class has opened my eyes to allow me to see the simple box I have lived in majority of my life." I've never had students ask me to recommend additional textbooks that they can read.

The great books are relevant and practical because they are the most intellectually challenging books that students can read. They provide the kind of complexity that cognitive scientists say is necessary to maintain brain health, promote learning, and stave off boredom.[20] Only they can support a curriculum that is both synoptic and precise, and produce "a necessary enrichment of intellectual character more quickly than alternative disciplines directed to the same object," as Whitehead says.[21] Only they, it is worth repeating, are broad enough for students to realize the intellectual depth of each. They allow students to wrestle with the essentials of any field directly while disciplining the mind, illuminating it, and teaching it how to reduce facts to order. As tools of instruction they combine both particular information and general knowledge with which liberal education aims to furnish the mind. They fulfill all the requirements of liberal education and reinforce the varieties of knowledge, the skills, and the habits of thought and mind appropriate to free and cultured human beings.

Allan Bloom has correctly pointed out that "wherever the Great Books make up the central part of the curriculum, the students are excited and satisfied, feel they are doing something that is independent and fulfilling, getting something from the university they cannot get elsewhere."[22] Taught and read properly, the great books turn us into masters of our intellectual tradition. More importantly, they turn us into masters of ourselves. What's needed is an undergraduate curriculum to match them.

CHAPTER 6

LAYERS OF READING

Books must be read as deliberately and reservedly as they were written.

~ Thoreau, *Walden*

The curriculum I propose is centered on the great books and taught in layers that correspond with the current stages of undergraduate education. It does not require overhauling existing curricula or doing away with majors or electives; it does require restructuring them so that the great books are truly its core. Students should take at least one great books course every semester of every year, although in the spirit of liberal education, more options should be available to adventurous and ambitious students. Each layer will emphasize new skills from the various levels of reading and reinforce skills that students have previously learned. Each great books course should reinforce knowledge acquired in other great books courses, as well as from other courses and students' majors.

The first layer of study will achieve two results. First, it will expose students to as many of the great books as possible; second, it will introduce them to the various levels of reading, elementary, inspectional, analytical, and synoptical, as Mortimer Adler describes in *How to Read a Book*. Elementary reading is basic literacy, the ability to recognize, interpret, and make sense of the symbols on printed matter. I will not discuss it here because it should have been mastered in grade school or high school at the latest, and therefore is inappropriate to undergraduate education.[1] I am also not suggesting—nor is Adler, I believe—that reading is formulaic, that by following a series of steps one will be transformed into a great reader; I am saying, however, as mentioned above, that reading is an intellectual activity that occurs on different levels and requires concentration, sustained effort, discrimination, and judgment. Or as Francis Bacon famously put it in his essay "Of studies:" "Some books are to be tasted, others to be swallowed, and some few to be chewed and digested: that is, some books are to be read only in parts, others to be read, but not curiously, and some few to be read wholly, and with diligence and attention." You probably already do this, but I think it is important nonetheless to be clear about the principles behind the various levels of reading so that we can turn our students into alert and heroic readers.

During their first year of study, students should be taught inspectional reading and the first stages of analytical reading. Initially every book—but especially the great books—should be read three times. The first reading is inspectional—better known as skimming—or trying to learn as much as possible about a book in the shortest amount of time. In my experience, students rarely (if ever) do this. When assigned a book (usually for the first time) they plough through it without considering what they are reading, rather than approach it like detectives on a crime scene, looking for clues about the book from the publisher's blurb, the Title Page and the Preface, the Table of Contents and the Index. They should ask and be able to answer rudimentary questions: What type of book is it? What is the genre? Who is the author? When was it written? Is it in English or a translation? Has it been edited? And so on. They should dip into it, turn its pages, and read a few passages or a couple of paragraphs or pages, but never more than that. Adler calls this "X-Raying" the book, or looking for those passages or chapters that might be important or pivotal to the author's argument. "Every book has a skeleton between its covers," he says, and it is the job of readers to find it. Inspectional reading informs readers how to approach a book so that they can read it analytically.

The second reading of a book is its first complete reading, and should be done swiftly, without resting or interruption, without "stopping to look up or ponder the things you do not understand right away." It is not necessary to explain everything or to expect students to remember all the details. In fact, the details are likely to be fuzzy, and the discussion superficial, because the material is new. (Those who fear superficiality should keep in mind Leo Strauss's advice: "There is no surer protection against the understanding of anything, than taking for granted or otherwise despising the obvious and the surface of things, and only the surface of things, is the heart of things." They should also remember that what seems deep or profound to them would be superficial to an author of a great book.) One should make sure that after the second reading students can classify or "pigeonhole" the book and state what it is about in a few sentences or a short paragraph.

By the third reading students should be familiar with the book and the "first difficulties" of reading it should be over, as Locke writes. At this point, "the delight and sensible advantage it brings mightily encourages and enlivens the mind in reading, which without this is very improperly called study."[2] Granted, this takes time and effort, but students should realize that the greater the book, the more it needs to be read all the way through, allowing time for synthesis and assimilation, for chewing and digesting. Reading with diligence and attention is the essence of analytical reading.

One way to encourage active reading at all levels, and to promote concentration and comprehension, is to get students to take notes on what they read. They should see no distinction between reading and studying. That means they must read with a pen or a pencil in hand; underline the major points and statements in the book; use vertical lines in the margins to emphasize passages that are too long to underline; mark the important points with asterisks or other symbols in the margins—or circle the page number; circle key words or phrases, or use different colored pens or highlighters; even count. Outlining is seldom taught these days, but it is still useful because it helps students to find the really important passages, delineate the major parts of the book, and show how these parts are organized into a whole, revealing the book's structure. Students should also be encouraged to write numbers in the margins to indicate the unfolding of an argument or several points that an author makes in sequence; and to write words or phrases in the margins ("slugs") to synthesize each important point of an argument or note their own questions or comments. Whether taking notes or outlining, they are making the book their own both physically and intellectually.

During the second layer of reading—either the second semester of the first year, or the first semester of the second year—the great books course should reinforce inspectional reading and advance the skills of analytical reading. Students should aim at comprehending and understanding some of the books they read during the first layer. This layer should emphasize (1) how to discover the author's meaning; (2) how to determine the author's message; (3) how to come to terms with the author. Students must first recognize the author's terms and address his problems or questions. A term is the "basic element of communicable knowledge," or as Adler defines it, a word "*used unambiguously*." A term may be jargon—the special vocabulary or technical words found in every field of knowledge—but not always. Jargon is bad when authors become too abstract, get lost in it, or use it to hide ignorance. Good writers understand that words refer to things (objects) and break down the barriers of language by clearly and distinctly defining their terms so that readers can comprehend their meaning. "The art of reading," writes Jacques Barzun, "consists in getting from the printed words as nearly as possible a sensation equivalent to the real thing," which readers have seen, heard, touched, tried to swallow, or whatever. "Without the image," he adds "the words remain only so much mumbo jumbo."

Of course it is up to readers to meet authors halfway, finding the words or phrases they use in special ways and identifying important key passages. Sometimes authors help by italicizing terms, or by putting them in boldface or in a different font; most often they do not. One reason the great books are difficult is that their authors often use terms that are alien to most modern readers. Therefore, it is crucial that teachers explain to students the importance of context in reading. They must show them how to discover the correct meaning of a word or a phrase they do not understand by using the meaning of all other words surrounding it that they do understand, or by using corroborative evidence, such as an author's correspondences or another great book, thus illuminating the tradition of learning and thought. When this happens, and they can explain the correct meaning, two minds share the idea, or possess a single thought, and the author is correctly understood.[3]

Having inspected the book and figured out the author's terms, students are now ready to find the propositions and arguments. Propositions "are nothing but expressions of personal opinion unless they are supported by reasons." Declarative sentences express them definitively, whereas interrogative sentences put them in the form of questions. They can be answers to questions, declarations of knowledge, or stated opinions. Teachers can help students find propositions or key sentences by selecting appropriate passages from the book and having them analyze each one as thoroughly as they can. This is what the French call *explication de texte*, in which students explain the meaning of a passage by producing everything they know. The effort should be cooperative, but teachers must guide their students, for example, by asking leading questions about the meaning of the words and sentences that express the author's judgments or support the arguments an author is making. The heart of an author's communication, writes Adler, "lies in the major affirmations and denials he is making, and the reasons he gives for doing so," and it is the teacher's job to show students how to discover propositions "by interpreting all the words that make up the sentence, and especially its principle words."

An argument is "a set or series of statements which provide the grounds or reasons for what is to be concluded" and is found in a book through connecting the key sentences. If the argument is not explicit, teachers must show students how to construct it "by taking a sentence from this paragraph, and one from that, until they have gathered together the sequence of sentences that state the propositions that compose the argument." In my experience, this is the most difficult exercise for students to do. It requires a discerning mind and judgment, since many sentences in a book are not part of the argument and students must be able to separate them from those that are important and support the argument. The difficulty is compounded when authors skip steps in an argument or use bad reasoning or faulty logic. "One of the most familiar tricks of the orator or propagandist,"

Adler warns, "is to leave certain things unsaid, things that are highly relevant to the argument, but that might be challenged if they were made explicit." Authors are typically more careful because printed matter is more easily scrutinized, although this is not always the case. We do not "expect such devices in an honest author whose aim is to instruct us," Adler adds, but "it is nevertheless a sound maxim of careful reading to make every step in an argument explicit." By identifying the important words, sentences, propositions, and arguments with students, teachers are both showing them and explaining how to interpret the book *from the author's point of view*.

In short, analytical reading engages students and develops habits of thought and mind by forcing them to read difficult books—but especially the great books—attentively and with care. It is their job to read with concentration, sustained effort, discrimination, and judgment.[4] They must use imagination, stop at every interesting and perplexing point, consult other books; they must walk around the room, wonder, and think; they must see that reading also means figuring out the book's character, looking for differences in what appears similar, and for similarities in what appears different; they must not skip over passages because what is boring or absurd or commonplace may reveal something profound or some clue that will lead to greater insight; they must pay attention to important points, contentious statements, obscure or ambiguous assertions, and unsupported claims; they must undertake a line-by-line analysis and see that every word has its place and meaning; if they cannot explain any detail, then their understanding is incomplete. This kind of rigorous reading, observes Locke, is what gives one person an intellectual advantage over another. Through constant use and exercise the mind becomes facile in the art of reading, so that "those who are accustomed to it, readily, as it were with one cast of the eye, take a view of the argument, and presently, in most cases, see where it bottoms." Those who possess this faculty, he adds, "have the true key of books, and the clue to lead them through the mizmaze of a variety of opinions and authors to truth and certainty." It is the proper way to show students how to profit from what they read.[5]

As teachers, our job is to guide students through the stages of analytical reading. We must show them how to attune themselves to the author's key terms, sentences, and paragraphs, and how to understand the context within which they are written so that students can discover the propositions and arguments in a book; we must help them to uncover the assumptions and self-evident propositions if they are not explicit, and to construct and summarize arguments, especially when they are not clearly stated; above all, we must show them that only after determining an author's message and meaning will they be in a position to make up their own minds, criticize a book fairly, and come to terms with an author's solution, the last two stages of analytical reading.[6]

The second layer of reading is also the time to introduce students to specific fields of inquiry within a great books context. Every subject has its classics around which an introductory course could be constructed. For example, in Anthropology, students could read E. E. Pritchard's *The Nuer*; Margaret Mead's *The Coming of Age*; Clifford Geertz's *The Interpretation of Culture*; Claude Levi-Strauss's *Tristes Tropiques*; Raymond Firth's *We the Tikopia*; R. F. Fortune's *Sorcerer's of Dobu*; Conrad Arsenberg and Solon Kimball's *Family and Community in Ireland*; Colin Turnbull's *The Forest People*; Victor Turner's *The Forest of Symbols*; and Laura Bohannan's *Return to Laughter*. A course on Latin America might focus on the writings (letters, diaries, logs) of Christopher Columbus and Amerigo Vespucci; Bernal Diaz del Castillo's *Conquest of New Spain*; primary document collections such as *Colonial Lives* and *Colonial Latin America: A Documentary History*; and Tzevetan Todorov's, *Conquest of America*. Students could study the principles of mathematics through Euclid's *Elements*, Nicomachus' *Introduction to Arithmetic*, Descartes' *Geometry*, Newton's *Principia Mathematica*, Peacock's *Treatise on Algebra*, Bertrand Russell's *Principles of Mathematics*, even Edwin Abbot's *Flatland*.

The benefit of approaching subjects in this way is threefold: first, it allows students to fulfill general education requirements—and might prompt some to pursue a given subject as a major; second, it fits the aim of liberal education by exposing all students to the various fields of inquiry essential for the cultured human being; third, and most important, it reinforces the skills of analytical reading and prepares them for synoptical reading, the highest and most complex form of reading emphasized in the third layer of undergraduate study.

Synoptical reading requires mastery of the other levels of reading because readers now use books for their own purposes. "Unless you know what books to read," writes Adler, "you cannot read synoptically; but unless you can read synoptically, you do not know what to read." With analytical reading, readers intend to learn something from a single book; understanding it is the goal. With synoptical reading, readers must determine whether several books say something relevant, meaningful, and useful about their subject; their concerns matter not the author's. Readers establish the terms and bring the author to bear on them, or as Adler says, they force the author to use their language, rather than using the author's. In short, the reader is in control. This does not mean distorting or misrepresenting what an author says; it does mean transferring an author's meaning—even constructing it from various passages—to state one's own propositions, answer questions, or address issues.

Adler lists five elements of synoptical reading: (1) finding the relevant passages; (2) bringing authors to terms; (3) getting the questions clear; (4) defining the issues; (5) analyzing the discussion. Synoptical reading builds on analytical reading because it requires defining the author's issues so that readers can objectively analyze and order the discussion to make their subject clear. Adler adds that the conscientious synoptical reader will "constantly refer back to the actual text of his authors" and read "the relevant passages over and over" so as to use them properly and accurately. More than the other layers of reading, synoptical reading develops discernment and judgment because students must select the relevant parts from appropriate sources for their own purposes. Seminars or special topics courses are probably best suited for teaching synoptical reading. Fewer great books will be read, and students can address a specific theme, concentrate on a progression of issues, and attempt to solve some problem, or answer a single question. Students address the four sets of questions of analytical reading:

- What is the book about as a whole? What is the leading theme of the book? How does the author develop it into topics and sub-topics?
- What is being said in detail, and how? What are the main ideas, assertions, arguments that contribute to the author's message?
- Is the book true, in whole or in part?
- What of it? What is its significance, relevance, usefulness?

Above all, they participate in the conversation among the authors of these great books, which reinforces the connections between the great books themselves.[7]

The fourth layer of study incorporates a capstone course or assignment. Under the supervision of someone not in their major, students choose a topic that will demonstrate how the great books relate to the subject of their major or to some other field of inquiry. For example, if they major in physics, they might consider Newton's biblical studies, which would show them how a mathematician and scientist dealt with theology and biblical criticism, as well as teach them some history. If they major in economics, they might apply some of the classics from psychology, sociology, or political science to think about why people choose to buy certain things, or whether consumers are as rational as classical economists would have us believe, thereby entering the conversation about human nature that one finds in almost every great book.

The combinations are limitless, as the authors of great books themselves reveal: Aquinas' knowledge extended to Scripture, philosophy, theology, law, even science; Hobbes mastered the Bible, argued with Aristotle, and relied on Bodin; even William James refers to Jane Austen in *The Principles of Psychology*. As Jacques Barzun writes, the "great philosophers and scientists are—or were until recently—universal minds, not in the sense that they knew everything, but in the sense that they sought to unite all they knew into a mental vision of the universe." The advantage for students is not only that they practice the methods of their field, but also that they show how their field is "interdisciplinary" and operates on assumptions from other fields of inquiry; the advantage for professors is that the subject matter and the texts will change from year-to-year, encouraging them to keep their own teaching fresh through exposure to texts from other fields, and prompting them to continue their own liberal education.

One result of my proposed revision to the undergraduate curriculum will be to teach students how to read. Professors, using their judgment, will evaluate students by considering such questions as these: Have they demonstrated their ability to read critically and with finesse? Do they know how to follow the lead of smooth prose, detect poor prose, pay attention to modifiers and transitions, keep ideas separate, interpret and comprehend what they have read? Can they follow arguments, the development of ideas, or distinguish between what an author actually says, or what someone else might say under similar circumstances? Can they explain something they have just read, or what an author means on any given point? Can they interpret a book and say what it is about without falling back on clichés? Have they developed discernment and sound judgment? Can they distinguish between "inferior" or easy books, difficult books, and great books? Are they capable of comparing master works with secondary sources, academic journals, and other lesser writings such as newspapers or magazine articles? In sum, what have they learned after four years? Are they "alert and heroic readers," or still as illiterate as those who have learned to read "only what is for children and feeble intellects," as Thoreau asks?

Another result will be that it supports the aims of liberal education. First, it encourages habits of reading and reinforces skills through the re-reading of certain books and various exercises. Second, it educates students by providing a link to the past and reinforcing the varieties of knowledge appropriate to the liberally educated human being. Third, it reestablishes the unity of knowledge and purpose that is missing in undergraduate education today; students will see that there is no such thing as an isolated subject and they will have before them models of universal minds that they can aspire to become or imitate. Fourth, it will prepare students intending to go to graduate or professional school through a rigorous curriculum; and it will satisfy Corporate America by teaching them the skills it now clamors for in college graduates—effective communication, critical thinking, ethic and civic responsibility, problem solving, quantitative literacy. Fifth, it will give students personal satisfaction from knowing that they can do something that they hadn't been able to do before, which Locke says is the essence of learning.

Yes, yes, critics will say—your proposal is quaint, but the whole scheme is superficial and impractical. It will demand more courses than students can reasonably take in 4 years. They will never have time to take great books courses in addition to electives and courses for their majors. Even if they do, the whole approach, if taken seriously, will demand a great deal of secondary source reading and it does not take into account recent advances in scholarship, current methods, or the latest knowledge, as the famous scholar of teaching and learning said to me. Otherwise you promote dilettantism and the unlearned self-assurance of the autodidactic, not competence or mastery of a particular body of knowledge.

Such objections miss the point because they miss the point of liberal education, which is broad instruction in the liberal arts that aims to imbue students with certain habits of thought and mind. My proposal intends to address the two problems endemic to undergraduate education today, of being either too broad and irrelevant on the one hand or too focused and specialized on the other. It will replace the smorgasbord approach to most undergraduate curricula today, which allow students to wander aimlessly in their studies, and perpetuate the condition described by George Bernard Shaw in his essay *Sham Education* (1931) in which "the crudest, darkest, poorest minds are allowed to propagate their crudity, darkness, and poverty." A curriculum is disastrous, he adds, when everybody "knows how to read and nobody knows what to read"—a point that modern cognitive science reaffirms: The "enormous size and the strict curriculum areas do little to help students find the time to make relevant connections between and among subjects."[8] When students are conscious of both the new learning and the context into which it fits, they are more likely to forge strong associations for future recall. While liberal education cannot be imposed, the virtue of a great books approach is that it does not waste students' time on inferior books; they will always be better off reading "the real authors, the men who have founded and discovered things" and "are recognized as the great masters in every branch of knowledge," as Schopenhauer says.[9]

My approach also solves the problem of an overly specialized undergraduate curriculum, which is equally disastrous, as Mark Van Doren has pointed out. The sad fact is that most undergraduate students, especially (but not exclusively) those in the sciences, begin and end their work "in total ignorance of what the greatest poets, critics, philosophers, mathematicians, scientists, statesmen, and moralists" have done before them. They might think it doesn't matter because their work is "new," but even the most specialized subjects are progressive and begin where someone else left off. "When those who are devoted to them forget this, they have lost the distinction between advancing knowledge and marking time."[10] Modern cognitive science likewise warns us against the tendency toward overspecialization: When "new learning is too tightly bound to the context"—such as when classes are too specialized, or when students think that grammatical correctness matters only in English courses—"then learners may fail to transfer that knowledge or skill to different contexts." A prescribed curriculum not only "encourages students to use their innate thinking abilities to process learning at higher levels of complexity," it teaches students "*how to organize content in such a way that it facilities and promotes higher-order thinking.*"[11]

Time will not be an issue because students will take only one great books course per semester. Nor will this approach demand any more secondary source reading than what is currently expected. Students will not be left to study the great books and learn on their own. Instructors will choose which books to read, as they do now, and can serve initially as secondary sources, providing advanced or expert knowledge where necessary. If teachers are attentive and imaginative they will turn questions that arise from reading them into useful exercises that get students to find the answers themselves—which they should be able to do once they leave college or university. In other words, they will teach them that reading aids learning through discovery, for "when all is said and done," Jacques Barzun reminds us, "one does not *teach a subject*, one teaches a student how to learn it."[12] Even in great books courses they can expose them to advances in scholarship, current methods, and the latest knowledge by pointing out differences and similarities between those in the great books and those of today. Perhaps I should reiterate once again that I am not suggesting we do away with majors or advanced courses that teach modern methods, but rather, in the interest of liberal education, that we do away with the absurd practice that every undergraduate course must be taught as if every student enrolled in it were majoring in the subject or intending to pursue it in graduate school.

Yes, yes, critics will say again—but you create more work for professors and take away valuable time from their own scholarship, which should be the basis of their teaching. Besides, they will get bored teaching the same books again and again. Perhaps. But preparing to teach a great books course will require no more work than is necessary for any other course—unless professors are recycling old material and not reading or doing anything new, in which case they are not using their own scholarship anyway and the point is moot. As for the relation between scholarship and teaching, the fact is that few undergraduate courses incorporate much of the scholarship that eventually finds its way into academic books and journals. My proposal will invigorate scholarship and preempt the kind of repetition that leads to boredom because teachers will be reading new books themselves to satisfy the curriculum. I agree that, under the current system, it is probably foolish for new professors to spend more time reading the great books because they need to research and publish to get tenure; but I also suspect that more graduate students and professors (new and old) would embrace a great books approach to the curriculum but are reluctant to admit it from fear of being branded as elitist, racist, sexist—or some other "-ist." Admitting to enjoy the great books in the current academic climate is like admitting to enjoy pornography.

Modern studies show that a prescribed curriculum like the one I'm proposing has an advantage over those commonly in place in colleges and universities in getting students to read and think critically.[13] Additional studies suggest that students may need at least 6 months before lasting effects and long-term enrichment begin to occur, and that they also need consistent contact with material in an appropriate environment for the nervous system to organize resources and respond accordingly.[14] A curriculum centered on the great books is more likely to achieve desired learning outcomes. Even if, as some maintain, the benefit of a prescribed curriculum is a result of smaller classes and active discussion that is typical of such programs, that only reinforces the value and need for more discussion that a great books curriculum promotes. Such changes could be made at little or no cost to colleges and universities, especially at a time when tuition is rising astronomically and more and more students are finding higher education unaffordable. Students will appreciate a curriculum based on the great books because they will pay less for the books required for their classes. Excellent translations and editions are usually available for around $10–20—or much less if you use Dover Thrift editions. I typically keep the total cost of books for my students under $100. Not surprisingly, the most expensive book they buy is the prepackaged textbook.

Another reason for a curriculum based on the close reading of great books is that it develops verbal expression and judgment, which require as much intellectual discipline and rigor as mathematical expression, as Charles Murray has demonstrated.[15] Verbal expression begins with the correct understanding of the meanings of individual words. This is followed by an understanding of the parts of speech, how they relate to the rules of grammar, and how sentences are structured to convey meaning—in a word, syntax. Reason and judgment, and their relation to language, play a part in verbal expression because they enable a person to recognize linguistic truths and fallacies, getting students to understand both "the distinction between *true* positions and *correct statements* of those positions," and "the distinction between *correct* statements of positions and *persuasive* statements of positions." Finally, verbal expression produces mastery of rhetoric, "both as a tool for expression and as a protection against being misled by rhetoric that is misused."

Since verbal expression is a tool for intellectuals and the managerial class—for example, for people in positions of power—we do a great disservice to our students by depriving them of the habits of thought and mind and the skills that will enable them to compete with their peers and advance in society. It is true, as Murray points out, that "learning verbal expressions is an advanced form is intellectually demanding work that only a small number of students can handle," and that "most students do not need to learn verbal expression in an advanced form" for what they do on a daily basis. But Murray also thinks that too many people are in college. And he may be right.

But the response of most colleges and universities is not. They have accommodated the growing numbers of students who are neither prepared for college life nor capable of doing college-level work by softening the curriculum and lowering standards, as the authors of *Academically Adrift* have made abundantly clear, and as students themselves are aware. A recent study shows that only 26% of undergraduates at small institutions, and only 18% at larger institutions, felt strongly that their professors had high expectations and challenged them academically.[16] At the state university where I taught, seniors taking my 100-level survey course told me that it was the hardest and most intellectually demanding class they had taken in 4 years at college! These students were actually grateful for having taken my course, and felt cheated by their other professors—although of course others weren't as grateful and eventually dropped the course and wrote negative comments on Ratemyprofessors.com. In an age when higher education exists for credentialing, and anyone can "get a degree," they wanted an easy professor and a blow-off class. I refused to accommodate them.

In the absence of a rigorous curriculum with demanding courses, such as those centered around the great books, it is up to us—as teachers on the front line—to restore integrity to higher education by imbuing our students with goals and aspirations consistent with broad instruction in the liberal arts.[17] We must not only demand higher standards from our students, we must show them that college-level work requires different levels of mastery than what they achieved in high school, even if their educational goals have nothing to do with acquiring a liberal education. But, you may say, students won't take my courses. That may be true, for a while. But in time, if you offer engaging and rewarding classes, from which students leave feeling like they have acquired useful knowledge and skills, and can do something that they were unable to do before, word will get out and they will sign up for them.

In many cases, in spite of my students' educational goals, I have succeeded, as one student clearly grasped, in getting them "to open their minds, and come to conclusions based on facts not fiction." He also said that I am the kind of professor colleges and universities need because I challenged him and other students "to do our own research so that we could come to class with thoughtful conclusions based on the material we were studying. This also went beyond the classroom," he added, because the experience allowed him "to start opening my mind to other corners of how the world works, and how I question what is true from what is not.

I noticed the same sentiment from other students around me. It was the first time I ever had a teacher who cared enough about the subject he was teaching along with his great concern that his students learned how to effectively learn new information." Above all, he "learned much about the subject, and even more about myself" because of the way I urged all "students to expand our minds." In fact, my student was willing to write all this, even though I "demanded a lot from [them] as a class."

The problem is not high standards. The problem is that too many professors are failing to maintain the standards for acquiring liberal education and to defend those standards across the curriculum—again, as the authors of *Academically Adrift* have also shown. Another problem is that faculty lack common goals about the ends of higher education and are inconsistent with their expectations from students in their courses. Nothing is more exasperating, in my opinion, than students, usually complaining about grades, who compare my standards with those of other professors. I refuse to go there, and flatly tell them that they are in my class not Professor X's. Some students, aware of my military background, have compared me with a drill sergeant, not only because of my high standards, but because I strictly enforce the rules that I put in my syllabus and lay down on the first day of class:

RUDE BEHAVIOR WILL NOT BE TOLERATED

- This includes:
    - sleeping in class;
    - talking while class is in session;
    - reading newspapers, letters, books, and other materials not related to the course;
    - working on other assignments during class;
    - using or checking mobile phones during class; and
    - texting or Twittering during class.

I have kicked students out of my classroom for violating these rules. But even in required courses with rigorous standards, reluctant students can be won over, as another told me in an e-mail at the end of a semester: "I wanted to let you know how much I enjoyed the course. I certainly entered with a bias against it, but found myself enjoying it more and more as the term progressed. You challenged me to think in new ways and question things I never would have thought to question before."

As teachers, we must cultivate in students the habits of thought and mind appropriate to free and cultured human beings who can think their own thoughts, experience beauty for themselves, and choose their own actions; we must imbibe them with the qualities of mind like skepticism, discipline, and judgment that will broaden their experience in the wider world. Locke was right when he wrote that liberal education aims not "to perfect a learner in all or any one of the sciences, but to give his mind that freedom, that disposition, and those habits that may enable him to attain any part of knowledge he shall apply himself to, or stand in need of, in the future course of his life."[18] The question is not what can we do, but *what are we willing to do* to achieve the aims of liberal education as a whole and promote genuine *synergy of learning* in our classrooms?

CHAPTER 7

WHAT'S WRONG WITH ACADEMIC WRITING

There is no such thing as good writing. There is only good rewriting.

~ Justice Louis Brandeis

Academics are notorious for bad prose, and in recent years, the editors of *Philosophy and Literature* have held a "Bad Writing Contest" to find the worst of it. Their aim has been "to locate the ugliest, most stylistically awful passage found in a scholarly book or article published in the last few years." Entries must be from actual serious academic journals or books. Some of the submissions are astounding. One winner was a sentence from Roy Bhaskar's *Plato etc: The Problems of Philosophy and Their Resolution* (Verso, 1994):

> Indeed dialectical critical realism may be seen under the aspect of Foucauldian strategic reversal—of the unholy trinity of Parmenidean/Platonic/Aristotelean provenance; of the Cartesian–Lockean–Humean–Kantian paradigm, of foundationalisms (in practice, fideistic foundationalisms) and irrationalisms (in practice, capricious exercises of the will-to-power or some other ideologically and/or psycho-somatically buried source) new and old alike; of the primordial failing of western philosophy, ontological monovalence, and its close ally, the epistemic fallacy with its ontic dual; of the analytic problematic laid down by Plato, which Hegel served only to replicate in his actualist monovalent analytic reinstatement in transfigurative reconciling dialectical connection,

---

The Skinny on Teaching: What You Don't Learn in Graduate School, pp. 87–105
Copyright © 2011 by Information Age Publishing
All rights of reproduction in any form reserved.

while in his hubristic claims for absolute idealism he inaugurated the Comtean, Kierkegaardian and Nietzschean eclipses of reason, replicating the fundaments of positivism through its transmutation route to the superidealism of a Baudrillard.

Yes, that's a single sentence. Or how about this one from an essay on "post-modern ethnography" by Stephen Tyler in *Writing Culture*, eds. James Clifford and George E. Marcus (California: University of California Press, 1986):

It thus relativizes discourse not just to form—that familiar perversion of the modernist; nor to authorial intention—that conceit of the romantics; nor to a foundational world beyond discourse—that desperate grasping for a separate reality of the mystic and scientist alike; nor even to history and ideology—those refuges of the hermeneuticist; nor even less to language—that hypostasized abstraction of the linguist; nor, ultimately, even to discourse—that Nietzschean playground of world-lost signifiers of the structuralist and grammatologist, but to all or none of these, for it is anarchic, though not for the sake of anarchy but because it refuses to become a fetishized object among objects—to be dismantled, compared, classified, and neutered in that parody of scientific scrutiny known as criticism.

Surprisingly, this kind of writing has defenders. In an essay in the *Times Higher Education Supplement* (November 2007), Professor Caroline Levine—who teaches English! at the University of Wisconsin-Madison—argues that "democracies need the very kind of difficulty represented by academic writing, and that they fail badly when they do not welcome these sorts of challenge." Academic prose may be difficult, uncomfortable, and strange to current sensibilities, but like avant-garde art it upsets "mainstream assumptions of the status quo" and "helps protect democracy from one of its own worst enemies—itself." But Professor Levine confuses issues. It's one thing to have complicated ideas; it's another thing to express them in indecipherable and muddled prose. Thomas Hobbes writes difficult and challenging ideas in *Leviathan*; but he proves that such ideas can be expressed clearly and distinctly, even in seventeenth-century English. Bhaskar and Tyler are simply bad writers.[1]

To be sure, not all academics write like them, but we still need to think about the effect that academic writing has on undergraduate teaching and the aims of liberal education. Even if we accept Professor Levine's point, the kind of writing exhibited by Bhaskar and Tyler is not the kind of writing that will serve students in the great world. What will serve them is writing that is plain, simple and direct. Almost every acute observer of the English language—from William Strunk and Sir Ernest Gowers to William Zinnser and Jack Lynch—agrees that this produces the best writing.[2] I think they would also agree that ordinary writing is what students should be taught, not academic writing, as many scholars of teaching and learning suggest. That does not mean it should be simplistic; it does mean that it should be free from verbiage, abstractions, clichés, euphemisms, unnecessary jargon, and pedantry; that it should be specific, definite, concrete, and clear above all else. Simplicity and plainness are virtues in writing as well as in life.

My concern in this chapter is not with the mechanics of writing—which, like elementary reading, ought to have been mastered at the lower levels—but with the elements that bear on teaching undergraduates to write, will promote verbal expression, and will inculcate the habits of thought and mind appropriate to the liberally educated person. As with reading, the place to begin is with words. Another reason the great books should be central to the undergraduate curriculum is that they force students to pay attention to words. "The proper signification and use of Terms," says Locke, "is best to be learned from those, who in their Writings and Discourse, appear to have had the clearest Notions, and applied to them their Terms with exactest choice and fitness."[3] With a little guidance, students who read even good books will become sensitive to the proper use of words and self-conscious about how to use them. The art of diction includes such features as understanding the bearing of words, their sound, their length, their connotations and suggestiveness, even their combination with other words. That means teaching students to use no more words than are needed to convey their message; to use words with precise meanings rather than vague ones; to use simple words when explaining complex ideas or technical terms. If two words convey their meaning equally well, they should choose the common one rather than the less common. At all costs they should write compact sentences and "omit needless words" (Strunk, Rule 13). As Gowers advises, "be short, be simple, and be human."[4]

Good writing is good manners because it always considers the reader. "A writer must make a sparing use of the reader's time, patience and attention," says Schopenhauer, "so as to lead him to believe that his author writes what is worth careful study, and will reward the time spent upon it." Understanding that words produce the quality and atmosphere of a piece of writing, good writers are exacting and try to imagine how readers will receive what they write. They will take time beforehand to figure out what they mean and find the words that fit. Good writers therefore avoid vague words, vogue words, woolly words, and clichés—the enemies of precision in writing and thinking; they are constantly on the lookout for malaprops and inappropriate expressions. I'm not saying that student writing—or even academic writing—must be judged by its literary quality; I am saying that it should be judged by its efficiency and clarity.

We all know that good writing uses the active voice over the passive voice; concrete words over abstractions; the familiar over the unfamiliar, for instance. We also know that good writing is forcible and precise, simple and direct. "If those who have studied the art of writing are in accord on any one point," writes Strunk, "it is on this, that the surest method of arousing and holding the attention of the reader is by being specific, definite, and concrete." The basics of plain English style promote the habits of thought and mind that we must imbibe in our students, who typically reveal in their writing the tendency of modern prose away from the features that produce it.

In a famous essay, "Politics and the English Language" (1946), George Orwell gives some reasons why. Bad writing results not only from the intention to deceive, but also from bad habits, staleness of imagery, and lack of precision, particularly in the use of words. Writing is weak when authors do not choose words for the sake of their meaning, when they repeat the words and ready-made phrases of others, or when they write as they speak. This saves mental effort, but it usually produces surplusage and vagueness. To tighten and clean up one's writing, Orwell recommends avoiding dying metaphors, abstractions, pretentious diction, and meaningless words. Scrupulous writers ask themselves at least four questions *in every sentence*: 1. What am I trying to say? 2. What words will express it? 3. What image or idiom will make it clearer? 4. Is this image fresh enough to have an effect? He includes two other questions that writers should also ask: 1. Could I put it more shortly? 2. Have I said anything that is avoidably ugly? Words must be both apt and correct to convey the author's meaning with precision. "In prose," Orwell adds, "the worst thing one can do with words is surrender to them."

As teachers we must eschew the inflated style of writing in both our students' prose and our own. Is it convoluted or unnecessarily complicated? Stilted or pedantic? Long-winded or circumlocutory? Full of clichés, euphemisms, or jargon? Can it be understood by the ordinary intelligent reader? Perhaps the most important question to ask is, How can we avoid—or rather, get our students to avoid—what acute observers of the English language warn us against?

First, we must teach them to prefer concrete words to abstract words. The reason to avoid abstractions is quite simply to make our meaning plain. "Many concrete words have a penumbra of uncertainty around them, and an incomparably larger one surrounds all abstract words," says Gowers. "If you use an abstract word when you might use a concrete one you are handicapping yourself in your task, difficult enough in any case, of making yourself understood." Abstract words often not only reflect imprecise thinking; they lead us to add others that are superfluous. The golden rule of writing is never to strain the reader.

Second, we must teach students to avoid verbiage—i.e., an "abundance of words without necessity or without much meaning" (OED). Just like passive sentences, certain words and phrases beget verbosity. Students are fond of writing *due to the fact that* when *because* or *owing to* will do. They write sentences that include phrases like *the question as to whether* when *whether* will do; *she was a woman who* when *she* will do; or *this is a subject that* when *this subject* will do. Other words, such as *very*, *really*, and *like*, should be used sparingly. So should adjectives and adverbs. "Cultivate the habit of reserving adjectives and adverbs to make your meaning more precise," adds Gowers, "and suspect those that you find yourself using to make it more emphatic. Use adjectives to denote kind rather than degree." For example, it is better to write an *economic crisis* or a *military disaster* than it is to write an *acute crisis* or a *terrible disaster*; and better to write a *careful study of* and *hardship* than an *in-depth study of* or *undue hardship*. The practice of writing with adjectives and adverbs, rather than relying on nouns and verbs, lends itself to overstatement and overemphasis, generating what Winston Churchill called "padding," meaning the "clumsy and obtrusive stitches on what ought to be a smooth fabric of consecutive thought."

Third, we must encourage students to choose familiar words over fancy words, foreign words, euphemisms, and jargon. "As in dress, it is pettiness to seek attention by some peculiar and unusual fashion," says Montaigne, "so in language, the search for novel phrases and little-known words comes from a childish and pedantic ambition. Would that I might use only those that are used in the markets of Paris!" I don't think that Montaigne or other acute observers of language would recommend using slang, which students should also avoid, but if it means being understood, then it is certainly preferable to mumbo jumbo and euphemisms, or to what George Carlin called "soft language."

The *poor* are now the *economically disadvantaged*; *cripples* now the *physically challenged*; *garbage men* now *sanitation engineers*; *secretaries* now *administrative assistants*. Such language is all around us, making it all the more pernicious. On a college campus where I taught, the weight room for athletes is called the *Strength Conditioning Center*; at another, Study Abroad is now *International Education*. I once saw a dermatologist's office called a *Centre for Skin Integrity* (note the pretentious British spelling). Unfortunately, modern scholars of teaching and learning promote such usage themselves. They talk about *active student learning* not simply *learning*; they have *outcomes* rather than *results* or *goals* or *aims*; they *assess* rather than *test* or *grade*. Now professors are referred to as professional educators (not teachers) and members of *academic communities* (not colleges or universities) who teach *disciplines* (not subjects or fields) employing *methodologies* (not methods). Pretty soon we'll be hearing about *professional educators* engaged in *teaching-centered instruction* and *research-centered scholarship*. The problem with such language is that it is pretentious and misleading, it is often used to hide ignorance, and it is always vague. People who write this way "usually have a general emotional meaning," observes George Orwell, but they "are not interested in the detail of what they are saying."

The same can be said about jargon, the special vocabulary or technical words in every field. In itself, jargon is not bad; indeed, it is useful as a shorthand to convey meaning and facilitate understanding. But as a rule of plain English style, it ought to be used sparingly or avoided altogether when it obscures meaning or becomes unintelligible to nonexperts. Think about this example: OMG ADIR TTUL. This is the kind of shorthand that students use in e-mails, text messages, and instant messaging; they've created their own language, or sub-language, with dictionaries.[5] What they write is perfectly intelligible to them, and justifiable as private communication, but it is unintelligible to outsiders and unjustifiable as external communication. We wouldn't accept this kind of writing in their papers or on their exams, and yet we expect them to follow our jargon and tolerate our academic speak. Both instances are inefficient and impolite as means of communication, and outsiders rightly feel excluded, puzzled, and annoyed. Overly technical or jargon-laden speech or writing will turn ordinary readers and students off, and those truly seeking enlightenment, says Gowers, "will find themselves plunged in even deeper obscurity."

You might think I am being unduly harsh, but such criticism of the pretentions of the learned is hardly new. Montaigne shared the bewilderment of the humanists over the convoluted Latin and inelegant writing of the Schoolmen and the lawyers in the sixteenth century: "Why is it that our common language, so easy for any other use, becomes obscure and unintelligible in contracts and wills, and that a man who expresses himself so clearly, whatever he says or writes, finds in this field no way of speaking his mind that does not fall into doubt and contradiction?" Locke warned against the "learned ignorance" of those who cannot frame their ideas clearly and distinctly but who try to convince us that they understand what they stand for and signify: "Words are not made to conceal, but to declare and show something; where they are by those, who pretend to instruct, otherwise used, they conceal indeed something, but that which they conceal is nothing but the ignorance, error, or sophistry of the talker, for there is, in truth, nothing else under them."

Bishop Berkeley pointed to another danger: "Unless we take care to clear the first principles of knowledge, from the embarrass and delusion of words, we may take infinite reasonings upon them to no purpose; we may draw consequences from consequences, and be never the wiser. The further we go, we shall only lose ourselves the more irrecoverably, and be the deeper entangled in difficulties and mistakes." More recently, Paul Fussell labeled language that combines "euphemism" and "grandiose syllable augmentation" as, not merely bad, but BAD. By BAD language he means the "impulse to deceive, to shade an unpleasant or promote the ordinary to the desirable or the wonderful, to elevate the worthless by a hearty laying-on of the pretentious." It is "so much the norm these days," he adds, "that there's virtually nothing said in public that, if both speaker and listener, writer and readers were honest and socially secure, couldn't be moved down toward a modest simplicity."[6]

What is new is the lack of a concerted effort among teachers and academics to combat the inflated style of writing and thought that Tocqueville says is characteristic of democratic peoples. The inconvenient truth is that academics contribute to it by using speech and writing prose that is often pretentious and verbose rather than plain, simple and direct, as Bhaskar and Tyler illustrate. They don't consider the danger that this manner of writing poses to writing in general, and they ignore that cause and effect reinforce each other, as George Orwell warned: "if thought corrupts language, language can also corrupt thought. A bad usage can spread by tradition and imitation even among people who should and do know better."

I suppose one reason for this kind of usage is insecurity, and perhaps even fear—the fear that ordinary readers might not take academics seriously if what they write doesn't appear complicated and technical; the fear that by writing simply other academics might think their work is simple too. (That's why I've always suspected that Somerset Maugham is not taken as seriously as he should be as a writer. He is so clear and compact that there is little wiggle room to quibble about what he says or means.) The message we need to send to our students is that people who really have something to say will always speak and write in the simplest and most straightforward manner, as Schopenhauer observed; intelligent people always use the more concrete way of expressing themselves because it "brings things more within the range of actual demonstration, which is the source of all evidence."

We also need to insist upon good ordinary writing in all our courses and throughout the curriculum. I don't know how many times I've heard students say when I tell them that their papers will also be graded on proper English usage, "This is a history class not an English class." Such statements underscore that they see education as a piecemeal rather than as a holistic undertaking and we must do everything within our power to dispel that notion. Like studying the great books, the practice of good writing must be a joint effort in which professors do not merely "enforce the rules" but "insure accuracy in every subject," including the sciences. Barzun's point is reiterated by physicist and Nobel laureate Sir Lawrence Bragg, who said that scientists must learn the gift of expression in plain, simple and direct prose, otherwise the "best research is wasted when it is extremely difficult to discover what it is all about." It is "even more important when scientists are called upon to play their part in the world of affairs, as is happening to an increasing extent." Good writing must reinforce both the aims and the unity of liberal education. If by precept and by example we taught our own students and persuaded other academics in our fields to write clearly, the "direct and indirect benefits" to writing "would be immense," as Gowers suggests. Perhaps more nonacademics would buy and actually read our books.

My intention is not to prescribe rules of writing for teachers to follow to a T, but to remind us to be vigilant about our students' writing—and our own. I'm suggesting that we need to teach writing in a way that also promotes genuine *synergy of learning*. One effective way is to teach writing through example by reading great or even good books analytically with our students. Reading teaches writing because it shows students what a thesis statement is and how to construct one, how to write appropriate sentences with exact words, how to organize those sentences into paragraphs and paragraphs into an argument that supports the thesis, how to make smooth transitions from point to point, how to write a conclusion, and how to use evidence properly and integrate quotations into one's prose. Professors must also explain the various techniques and styles of the authors of the books they use. Then they must give students assignments that force them to practice these techniques and develop their own style. Finally, they must supply rigorous criticism of their writing and guidance making substantial revisions to their papers. This is nothing more than the old method of actually instructing students—i.e., showing them how to write by commenting extensively on their papers or going over them during tutorials or classroom discussions.

For example, I often assign Martin Luther's *On the Freedom of a Christian* (1520), not only because it is appropriate for my survey and upper-level courses, but also because it provides students with an excellent example of how to write persuasively and argumentatively. In addition to asking students questions about the text itself, as described above, I have them outline the essay so that they understand how Luther has structured his argument, and so that they will pay attention to how he writes. Luther knows he is walking a fine line. He is in the midst of a bitter religious controversy and, in a shrewd and bold move, dedicates his treatise to Pope Leo X, although he is clearly attempting to explain and justify his position to a larger audience. In a brilliant example of expository writing, he uses the tools of rhetoric to say one thing but suggest something very different, and the tools of logic, reason, and evidence to argue his points.

In the Dedicatory Letter, he claims that he is not attacking the pope personally but rather the enemies of piety who surround him. He compares the pope to Daniel in the Lion's den, says that Rome itself has been corrupt, and that his purpose in writing this essay is actually to defend Leo from flatterers and the enemies of peace. In fact, Luther goes so far as to say that he is Leo's friend and that what he writes comes from his sense of duty as a Christian. But when he refers to the Court of Rome as a "disordered Babylon," he is making a veiled attack against a corrupt church and the pope through an allusion to Petrarch's characterization of the Avignonese Papacy as the "Babylonian Captivity" and the pope as the "whore of Babylon." Luther apologizes for being "shamelessly bold in seeming to teach so great a head, by whom all men ought to be taught," but his essay is didactic in that it provides a "summary of the Christian life put together in small compass," that is, if the pope can "apprehend its meaning." On the one hand, Luther is addressing Leo, whom he is trying to persuade that he is a true Christian; on the other hand, he stands his ground and maintains the position of justification through faith alone, which got him into trouble in the first place. Luther knows that he is undermining essential dogmas of the Catholic faith itself, and probably never expected the pope to accept his apology; but he has a platform, and takes advantage of it to provide a new definition of what it means to be a Christian. The rest of the essay shows this.

Analyzing the essay with my students, my aim is to get them not only to see why Luther is a seminal figure in the Protestant Reformation, thus teaching them content, reinforcing the broader themes of my course, and connecting their readings with other great books; but also to see *what Luther is really saying* and *how he is saying it*. In other words, my aim is to teach students how to write persuasively and argumentatively through imitation and example (even though they are reading a translation). In addition, I get them to see how Luther uses the tools of rhetoric to advance a position that contradicts what the Catholic faith upholds. While discussing and outlining the essay with them as a class, I show them Luther's logical and orderly structure, as well as his tight and methodical reasoning. Having identified Luther's thesis, I show them how he supports that thesis with examples, arguments, and evidence from the Bible (and of course we discuss the nature of his evidence). I also show them where Luther takes into account what his detractors say, or poses the counter arguments to his position, an essential feature of good writing. Finally, I get them to imitate what they have learned in their own essays.

Since I also often assign Machiavelli's *The Prince* and More's *Utopia* in survey and upper-level courses, I require students to demonstrate their understanding of the subject and mastery of the content by comparing and contrasting these sources and placing them within the appropriate historical context. I might ask them something like the following:

> Both humanism and the Protestant reformation have been called revolutionary intellectual movements. Using specific examples and citing evidence from Machiavelli's *The Prince*, More's *Utopia*, and Luther's "On the Freedom of a Christian," compare and contrast the overall effect of these two movements on European society from the fourteenth to the sixteenth centuries. How do these writers represent a radical break with the Middle Ages?

I make it very clear to my students that will be graded on, among other criteria (such as page length and citation format), their mastery of plain English style. That means practicing good grammar and proper English usage, paying attention to content and organization, using evidence and making arguments, developing consecutive thought, writing persuasively and argumentatively by proving a thesis.

To help them, I offer to tutor students in my office, but invariably few show up for help. So I've begun asking them to submit their introductory paragraphs in advance, from which I select two or three to review in class. I split students into groups and ask each group to tell the rest of the class what is good or bad about the paragraph and why. (Beforehand I have assigned appropriate sections from Strunk and Lynch, which they must use while explaining their reasons.) Having already discussed the primary sources, and now these paragraphs, students have concrete models before them of what I expect and consider good writing as they write their papers. After the papers have been turned in and graded, I select one good paper and one bad paper, post them online for the students to print and bring with them to class, and assign additional relevant sections from Strunk and Lynch to guide their critique these papers. Then, as we have done before with the introductory paragraphs, we review them together as a class. This not only allows me to reinforce the elements of good writing, it provides additional concrete instruction from which they should benefit for the next assignment. More recently, I have begun assigning two or three shorter papers using this method as a means to prepare students for their first major writing assignment, usually a take-home mid-term exam.

In this way, course readings serve my students as books did for Montaigne, "not so much for instruction as for exercise."[7] They promote genuine *synergy of learning* and reinforce the habits of thought and mind appropriate to the liberally educated person. In this way, too, they reinforce the skills of ordinary writing that they learned (or should have learned) in English Composition in high school or Expository Writing during their freshman year. This old method of teaching writing works just fine, provided that teachers take time to instruct their students by giving them the attention they both need and deserve. "Once past the essentials," William Strunk observes, "students profit most by individual instruction based on the problems of their own work." Indeed, my own experience bears this out, as a second-year student told me: "Through your insight and guidance, I feel that I have written one of the strongest papers of my academic career thus far." And so do modern studies.[8] Summing up the data, Derk Bok has pointed out that progress in writing depends mostly on "how much writing students did, how much specific feedback they received, whether they wrote about something they knew a lot about, and whether their subject let them bring their own intellectual interests into their composition." Like critical thinking, good writing "will never be a skill that students can achieve or retain through as single course."[9]

But too many in academe, including some modern scholars of teaching and learning, have turned their backs on the old method and the result is that college students are not learning to write, as they themselves acknowledge. In a recent study of 30,000 undergraduates at 26 selective colleges, fewer than 50% felt that their writing had improved over four years. And in a study of 24,000 students at larger institutions, only 27.6% saw improvement in their writing. Yet 80% of the students surveyed felt that they would have become better writers if they had received more feedback from their professors and had more direct contact with them. Part of problem, says Derek Bok, is that administrators think writing is "easy," a matter of purging students of bad habits, so they have pawned off most writing classes to graduate students or adjuncts. By the 1990s more than 95% of all required writing courses in PhD-granting English departments were not taught by full-time faculty. That's the other part of the problem. Professors don't want to deal with this. They are hired to research and publish, not to teach students to write, which is time-consuming, as my own example above shows.

Granted, students are more likely to encounter this attitude at big institutions, but it is becoming more common at smaller schools and community colleges, especially as class sizes keep rising and faculty are under pressure to research and publish. The great irony of higher education is that the more teaching is emphasized at an institution, the more students and classes a teacher gets. At community colleges faculty typically teach a 5/5 load with as many 175–200 students per semester, and even at smaller schools faculty carry a 3/3 or 4/4 load with as many as 80–125 students per semester.[10] Common sense would dictate the opposite. Professors who mostly care about research, and students who mostly care about getting the degree, should be put in large courses where the professor simply lectures and students take multiple-choice exams; whereas professors who care about teaching, and students who want to learn or need the most help, should be put in smaller classes where they will benefit from individual attention.

Although programs such as Best Practices in Writing and Writing Across the Curriculum have been around since the 1970s, with some success, their proponents can't agree on "the best" or most effective method to teach writing.[11] Gerald Graff and Cathy Birkenstein have offered another approach in *They Say, I Say: The Moves That Matter in Academic Writing* (W. W. Norton, 2006), which was required of all freshman taking Liberal Studies at a college where I taught. Their self-proclaimed goal is to write a "user-friendly guide to the basic moves of academic writing," by which they simply mean a book on argumentative writing. To argue well students must do more than assert their own ideas, they must "enter a conversation, using what other say (or might say) as a launching pad or sounding board" for their own ideas. "For this reason, one of the main pieces of advice in this book is to write the voices of others into your text." The "best academic writing" is always "deeply engaged in some way with other people's views."

No doubt this is true, but they recommend teaching students to write by using templates, which they claim are "the most distinctive" and "popular" feature of their book. Distinctive and popular to whom? My students hated them. Not a single student told me that she felt she was learning to write clearly and distinctly in the plain English style by mechanically incorporating such phrases into her prose as these from an Index of Templates: *Americans today tend to believe that ...* or *When I was a child, I used to think that ...* or *So far we have been talking about ... but isn't the real issue here....* As one student complained, "People don't write like that." She then went on to compare this way of teaching writing to the way she had been taught to converse in Spanish in high school through the memorization of phrases, and added, "People don't speak like that." Templates went against her natural instincts and reinforced her view that everything academic is artificial and stiff. What advocates of methods like these lose sight of is that writing is largely a matter of taste and judgment which must be cultivated through practice, experience, and extensive reading. They ignore the fundamental principle of teaching and learning, as I described it above, that instruction works best when it starts with a particular concrete experience and works toward the general.

This is precisely what the 2006 Report of the National Committee on Writing concluded: "Genuine teaching and learning are intensely personal, not scripted, participants agreed. They take place when minds engage around substance. Research confirms that learning is always academically rigorous and relevant—and individualized in the sense that it connects students with adults in work designed to meet young people's academic and developmental needs." In a similar vein, Peter Smagorinsky, professor of English at the University of Georgia, suggests that the quality of writing instruction depends on "the particular people who come together to teach and learn and the qualities of whatever precedes and surrounds them in the setting of the classroom." Because people develop different worldviews, they learn and think differently; therefore, teachers must employ a variety of skills and approaches in accord with their own—and their students'—training, dispositions, experiences, and other factors.[12] This doesn't mean we have to embrace Smagorinsky's instructional relativism; it does mean we must recognize that teaching writing—like teaching in general—is an art that requires dexterity and finesse and the ability of teachers to see and understand its relation to individual students and liberal education as a whole.

But that is what books like *They Say, I Say* do not do. Rather than teach writing by getting students to imitate the writing of good writers—as I try to do with my Luther assignment—they mechanize both the teaching and the practice of writing by reducing it to rules devoid of context; in consequence, they detach writing from other activities and courses that students undertake. Imitation is one thing; formulaic writing is another. It's the same kind of pedantry that sucked all the life out of classical Latin during the Renaissance. It's the scholarship of teaching and learning mentality that the mechanization of method can solve the problem of poor student writing in an age of mass education. To write well, students must know how to think; to learn to think, they must know how to read. Our concern should be turning them in competent thinkers, readers, and writers.

Instead, we turn them into pedants. Academic writing also means teaching students to imitate the way academics write—grafting one authority upon another, rehashing arguments, padding papers with numerous citations, references, and bibliographies. Of course documentation and evidence are important, they are the staples of scholarship, but we are encouraging students to play at scholarship before they know how to think, read, and write. Even worse, they adopt the manners of expression of scholars because they want to appear learned. But it's showiness. It says, "Look at me. I sound like Professor X and Professor Y." What Montaigne asked in the sixteenth century could still be asked today: "Is it not the chief and most reputed learning of our times to learn to understand the learned? Is that not the common and ultimate end of all studies?" Nothing can be said unless it has already been acknowledged by some contemporary academic. We've created a new Scholasticism.

This kind of pedantry is no different from the pedantry of strictly adhering to every grammatical rule, such as forbidding students to split infinitives or end sentences with prepositions. It's what makes a great deal of modern writing unnatural and stiff, what provoked Kingsley Amis to say to American authors: "*Come off it*, off your stilts, off your high horse. Be natural for a change, which is not the same thing as being colloquial or writing in a 'pure' style, but beware of writing in any special writing way, a way that you would never speak. Writers seldom write just as they speak, but they move away from their speaking voice at their peril."[13] Learning should be worn loosely, like a good suit or pair of trousers: they fit and they are comfortable; people see them on you but take no particular notice of them. It is misplaced to teach undergraduate students to think and write like academics when most do not intend to become academics themselves. Roger Ascham, a famous sixteenth-century educational theorist and scholar little read today, anticipated Amis's useful advice: "He that will write well in any tongue, must follow this counsel of Aristotle, to speak as the common people do, to think as wise men do; and so should every man understand him, and the judgment of wise men allow him." So did Schopenhauer, who said that even the genius should "talk the same language as everyone else" and "use common words to say uncommon things." Once more we have the wrong emphasis, and would be better off following the sound methods of the great masters.

To sum up, students should be taught not academic but ordinary writing, by which I mean writing that is plain, simple and direct. They should observe the rules of standard usage, but at this stage worry less about the mechanics than about imitating good writing from the books they are reading with teachers. They should pay attention to words and convey their meaning without ambiguity or unnecessarily troubling readers. They should follow Gowers's three basic rules of usage:

- use no more words than are necessary;
- use familiar rather than far-fetched words; and
- use words with a precise meaning rather than those that are vague.

To these we might add Orwell's six rules, which they should also follow:

- never use a metaphor, simile, or other figure of speech which you are used to seeing in print;
- never us a long word where a short one will do;
- if it is possible to cut a word out, always cut it out;
- never use the passive where you can use the active;
- never use a foreign phrase, a scientific word, or a jargon word if you can think of an everyday English equivalent; and
- break any of these rules sooner than say anything outright barbarous.

Clarity is the aim of all writing, and clarity depends on finding exact words. I'm not saying that students should write with a thesaurus in hand, which can also generate pedantic and stilted prose, but that words are the basic stuff of writing. Right words in the right places, says Swift, is the essence of style.

But why do we write? I think this is one question we neglect to ask our students—and perhaps even ourselves. The answer, of course, is to be read. Like teaching, writing is less of a chore, and actually gratifying, when you love your subject and are so enthralled by it that you must convey your thoughts and ideas to others. Good writers, like good teachers, usually feel compelled to communicate the magic, as bestselling and Pulitzer Prize-winning author Barbara Tuchman once said. A self-proclaimed writer whose subject was history, she preferred talking about the problems of writing, "not only because they interest me more but because the average layman underrates writing and is overimpressed by research." Many readers said to her in awed tones: "Think of all the research you must have done!" What they didn't realize was that research is the easy part, and endlessly seductive; writing takes twice as long and is much harder work.[14]

I don't think that many undergraduate students see writing as difficult work. It's something they think they can do, like reading, and therefore feel little or no compulsion to put much effort into their papers to make them pleasurable to read. They don't consider that their papers may actually be a nuisance or boring to us. If there is drudgery in our work, it is grading, and I have yet to meet a teacher who looks forward to grading papers or exams. We have about as much excitement reading our students' papers as they have in writing them. They approach papers as papers, hoops to jump through to pass the course, but don't believe in the importance of what they are doing or saying. "He who writes carelessly," Schopenhauer points out, admits that "he does not attach much importance to his own thoughts." We detect their insincerity and reluctantly do our duty. We play at writing rather than take it seriously and encourage our students to do likewise. We must strive to make writing an activity in which students want to convey something.

One thing we can do, as I said earlier, is to show them that a subject has personal value and makes them feel like something important is at stake. And nothing is more personal than writing. Have them participate in choosing the paper topics or ask them occasionally to write less formal papers. In one class I gave students the option of choosing the format—a story or a dialogue or a short play, for instance—to discuss how old-man Montaigne would respond to Romeo and Juliet. (We had read Montaigne's essay "On some verses of Virgil" and Shakespeare's *Romeo and Juliet*.) Several students who chose this option wrote creative essays. For example, one had Montaigne and Romeo and Juliet appearing on "The Oprah Winfrey Show"; another pretended that Montaigne was a marriage counselor being visited by these two adolescent lovers; another rewrote scenes of the play inserting Montaigne in key parts. The aim was to get them to write an essay that would be interesting for them to read—and still incorporate the elements of good writing mentioned above. They enjoyed writing these essays and did much better on them than they did on their first formal essays.

Perhaps it goes without saying, but before we can make writing personal we must prepare students to write by making sure that they have mastered the subject matter. Then they must do all the preliminary work, distill all relevant information, assemble it so that it makes sense to the reader, construct arguments. "One proves something by showing whether arguments are strictly cogent or not," says Aristotle. "Not all facts can form the basis of an argument, but only those that bear on the matter in hand." Here the skills of analytical and synoptical reading are put to use. Selection is everything. Even modern cognitive scientists tell us this: "Getting information is essential for learning.... The data collected by the sensory neocortex are like bits that, by themselves, have no useful meaning. *Learning is not equal to data collection*" (italics added).[15] Students should never leave a mass of undigested facts for readers but assemble them in such a way that they persuade as well as please. Part of the challenge—and fun—of writing is developing an "ear" for what you are writing, enthralling your readers, making your subject captivating though corroborative details and dramatic construction. Without these writing is bald and unconvincing rather than vivid and memorable. The question all writers should keep before them is: "Will the reader turn the page?"

Another thing we can do to make writing an activity in which students want to convey something, is to get them to pay attention to tone, style, and meaning. Words generate tone because they are a manifestation of attitude and betray what we feel or think. Tone is typically revealed in sentences and paragraphs and it usually determines whether a reader eagerly or drudgingly turns the page, or stops reading altogether. The proper tone will "convert a flabby style into a crisp one," suggests Gowers, and style is the most personal part of writing. Montaigne often read for style because through it he got to know the author; Schopenhauer called style the physiognomy of the mind. But style is not ornament, and those who write for adornment often produce affected prose, such as students who try to write like academics. Their tone is staid and their style stilted rather than natural, vigorous, and forcible.

Saul Bellow once said that the American style in writing comes from speech, by which he meant—like Montaigne, Schopenhauer, and Amis—that it should be natural and unaffected. Somerset Maugham, one of the greatest writers of modern English prose, says that good writing possesses lucidity, simplicity, euphony, and liveliness. If your writing displayed these four virtues, "you would write perfectly: you would write like Voltaire."[16] A good style should show no sign of effort but should be all ease and precision and grace. It is as much the same thing as good manners in other human intercourse, that is to say, you consider your readers, thinking of them instead of yourself and endeavoring to make yourself clear. Good writing will have unity, coherence, and clarity above all else. Clarity, clarity, clarity.... I tell my students. It is better to be simple and clear and understood than clever and confusing. Say what you mean to mean what you say. Together words and tone and style make it easy or difficult for readers to comprehend your meaning.

Still another thing we can do is to get students to revise their work, not once but several times. Schopenhauer reminds us that "nothing is easier than to write so that no one can understand" and "nothing is more difficult than to express deep things in such a way that everyone must necessarily grasp them." The whole point of attuning students to words is to become self-conscious about language and to develop the habit of self-criticism. Practicing the art of diction will give them control over their thoughts and promote ownership over their ideas and writing. Good writing means easy reading, and revision is the path to good writing. It gives writers the opportunity to say exactly what they mean as forcibly as they can. "Read and revise, reread and revise, keep reading and revising until your text seems adequate to your thought," advises Jacques Barzun, who lists several questions that we should train students to ask themselves:

- What is the tone of my piece?
- Does the prose move satisfactorily?
- Is each statement exact and clear?
- Is each sentence properly constructed?
- Is each word appropriate?
- Does each correctly convey my meaning?
- Do my ideas appear in consecutive order and flow?
- Is each point adequately addressed?
- Is my introduction engaging and my conclusion satisfactory?
- Have I overlooked anything?[17]

We might add another question: Am explaining too much? It is boorish to say everything, suggests Voltaire.

Strictly speaking, we cannot teach our students to write, but we can help them to become better writers by assigning good books in our courses and by our criticisms, suggestions, and guidance. It is not enough to write *awkward* or *rewrite* in the margins or to circle words or phrases; we must suggest better words or phrases, recast sentences for them, point out illogical constructions of sentences and paragraphs, explain what is wrong with their papers with lengthy comments in the margins and a summation at the end—in short, we must tutor them. Students often make common mistakes so many problems can be addressed orally to the entire class. Hand out samples and discuss them with your class. Point out errors or bad writing and explain why they are errors or bad; this will both instruct and prevent them from making the same mistakes later on.

I've even adopted peer critiquing in my classes. Students pair up and read their papers aloud to other students, who address issues that concern the author and answer questions about the paper that we've come up with together as a class. This exercise not only eliminates many common annoyances, such as misspelled words and awkward phrases, it gives students practice revising their papers, which they almost never do. After the peer critiques I let them rewrite their papers before they submit them for grading. (They must turn in the original with the corrected version.) No one is asking students to fuss over their essays like Flaubert, who sometimes spent hours or even days working to perfect his sentences, but we should emphasize that papers written a few days or the night before will invariably be bad and that writing will improve only through rigorous self-criticism and substantial revision.

I realize that there are obstacles to my suggestions. Classes are large, there are too many students, and all this revision takes time—time both students and professors would rather spend doing something else. Students have other courses, extracurricular activities, and social lives to worry about; professors (especially new ones) must prepare courses, serve on committees, advise students, and of course research and publish for tenure and promotion. Another obstacle is the snobbery of some professors who think they shouldn't have to stoop to perform remedial work—that's what teaching assistants and writing centers are for. Still another obstacle is instruction without authority, the coddling that is prevalent in colleges and universities today. We are afraid to criticize students. We don't want to hurt their feelings. They might feel slighted or inadequate or inferior if we return marked-up papers to them. They might take it too personally. So we let things slide, and our students are worse off for it. They get to graduate school or take jobs where their supervisors are astounded that they can't write clear and distinct prose, costing American corporations as much as $3.1 billion annually, as noted earlier.

But what are we there for? These obstacles are symptoms of the real problem in higher education today: Teaching is not important. The simple fact is that writing would improve if professors at all levels spent more time actually teaching it—and of course practiced writing plain, simple and direct prose themselves, as the National Commission on Writing recommends: "More attention must be paid to writing. More time must be found for it. And teachers must be provided with the time and resources required if they are to perform their work professionally."[18] More attention would also reduce the plague of plagiarism because, by taking time to get to know our students and how they think, we would be able to detect if their style reflected their personality and character. Students won't write like Mary Shelley or F. Scott Fitzgerald because they don't think like them. If we did our jobs we wouldn't need Turnitin.com or such other web sites. Instead, we've made a calculated decision not to. It's just not worth it. It's easier to ignore the problem or pretend that we're teaching them how to write, pass them in our class, and get on with our own work. True to form, scholars of teaching and learning have devised another mechanized solution to the problem of bad undergraduate writing: the grading rubric. Rubrics are convenient—I use them myself—but let's not fool anyone. They are a facade. They merely give the impression of "objectivity" and serious evaluation but are nothing more than checklists devoid of substantive criticism and judgment. Their real purpose is to save time.[19]

If colleges and universities were serious about teaching students to write well, professors would be evaluated on their students' graded papers, which would become part of hiring, tenure, and promotion. Teachers would be required to submit an entire class's worth of papers over several semesters or years to show the kinds of comments and critical reading that they have done. This would evaluate more judiciously how they actually teach writing because it would show the progression of assignments and substantive criticisms—or lack of them. Their evaluators would judge them at their tasks in the same way teachers evaluate students at theirs. Teachers would certainly be more conscientious about grading if they knew that getting a job or tenure or promotion depended on it. It would stop both teachers and students from playing at writing—and students might actually be grateful and flattered that their teachers took what they wrote seriously.

Until that happens, it is again up to us—as teachers on the front line—to promote better writing among students. We can begin immediately with these three steps: first, we can do away with multiple-choice exams, which do not test knowledge or understanding but the ability to memorize and recognize facts; second, we can do away with assignments that require only factual answers; third, we can do away with jejune exercises like book reports in which students regurgitate what someone else has written.[20] I would even advise doing away with research papers, at least at the lower levels. "Size being aimed at," writes Jacques Barzun, "there is no time for rewriting or reordering the material culled from half a dozen books, and the main effort goes into the irrelevant virtues of neat typing, plentiful footnotes, and the mannerisms of scholarship." Research papers encourage students to play at scholarship, as I mentioned above, and are usually unoriginal and unreadable. Very rarely do undergraduate students demonstrate the ability or have adequate time to investigate a topic closely, and they almost never have access to the sources that permit undertaking these enormous projects. Besides, professors who encourage undergraduates to write lengthy research papers are usually those who wish they had graduate students but don't; or they have graduate students but don't like teaching undergraduates, so they treat them like graduate students. There's no point of trying to turn undergraduate students into specialized scholars.

Like reading, writing means thinking, and teaching it properly and effectively is an essential part of undergraduate education. It must be taught not merely as a set of skills to be mastered but concretely as a tool of the mind that gives students real power and the ability to express their own thoughts and ideas. The rules and precepts of standard usage must be reinforced at all levels of learning because they make students aware of what to look for, practice, improve, and imitate. As teachers we must eschew the modern tendency away from prose that is plain, simple and direct. We must practice the habits of good writing ourselves, which is nothing more than practicing the habits of thought and mind appropriate to the liberally educated person.

CHAPTER 8

HOW *WE* CAN SAVE LIBERAL EDUCATION

After all our studies we acquire only that which we put into practice.

~ Goethe

At the end of one semester, as I was passing out the final exam on the last day of a class, a student asked if I had any parting words of wisdom, another life lesson that he and the others could take with them into the great world. I stopped passing out exam, stood straight up, and smiled to myself as I thought, "Do I tell him what I really think?" I knew I'd never see him or the other students again. The chair of my department had informed me a few weeks before that the dean was replacing me with a couple of adjuncts the following year. Although a visiting assistant professor, I was chosen for the position because the department anticipated it would become a tenure-track line the following year. But the economy tanked, budgets needed to be cut, and the administrators of my university did what administrators across the country typically do to stay in the black. I told my student, "Don't become a teacher or have anything to do with education. It's a racket."

Perhaps my response sounds bitter, after all I had lost my job, but I don't think that I was expressing any more cynicism or discontent than what already prevails in the profession.[1] In truth, it came from a deeper concern that, as a teacher, I might be disingenuous in promoting liberal education

---

The Skinny on Teaching: What You Don't Learn in Graduate School, pp. 107–111
Copyright © 2011 by Information Age Publishing
All rights of reproduction in any form reserved.

as a worthwhile goal for my students. Henry Adams wrote an entire book to show how traditional education failed him. Saul Bellow satirized the uselessness of a liberal education in the novel *Herzog*. Former Yale professor William Deresiewicz calls his a "miseducation" that brought numerous disadvantages, among them an inflated sense of self-worth and the inability to talk to people who were not like him.[2] Why should I expect students to take me seriously when I tell them that liberal education is a worthwhile pursuit?

And yet I still believe in liberal education and its transformative power, and that life as a scholar-teacher is a great privilege, otherwise I wouldn't have written this book. I think of my own experience, about the experiences of some of my students whose lives have been changed because of it, and more to the point, about the experiences of those whose lives haven't been. When my brother-in-law died of a heart attack at age 49, my sister, who had never been to college, who had spent her entire adult life working and raising her sons and building a solid home for her family, was confronted with the meaning of life in the most immediate and profound way. She began asking herself for the first time the kinds of questions that are central to liberal education and part of its intellectual and spiritual journey: Who am I? What can I know? What may I hope? What is it all about? What ought I to do? I'm not saying that a liberal education would have given her answers to these questions, but it would have given her perspective and put her on the right path to find answers to them. Instead, my sister looked helpless and unsure where to turn. The outcome of liberal education may be immeasurable, and its value intangible and nonmaterial, but that doesn't make it any less meaningful or real. I'm not so naïve as to think that liberal education will solve all our problems, in higher education or in life; but like our democracy, it's the best system we've got, and worth preserving.

Here, then, are five additional things that we can do to restore the idea of higher education. First, we can stay engaged professionally. This means not only continuing to study our subjects and mastering our specialties, but also reading as widely as possible in other subjects, particularly the primary sources; it means reconsidering the fundamentals from time to time, rechecking premises, going through demonstrations, questioning and reevaluating our assumptions; it means reexamining the ultimate principles of our subjects, extending boundaries by raising new questions and posing new answers; it means being self-critical, avoiding prejudice, rethinking lectures and strategies for classroom discussion, never letting them become mechanical by regurgitating the same information year after year; it means maintaining our vitality as teachers, whether through sabbatical, changing topics, developing new courses, reading afresh the books we continue to use, or choosing new books; above all, it means reading the classic texts on education, thinking about teaching at both its practical and theoretical levels, and constantly striving to improve our performance in the classroom. This is the essence of scholarship, which is not the same thing as researching for the sake of publishing.

Second, we must refuse to throw up our hands and surrender to administrators and the pressure to become overly specialized researchers. We must strive to convince colleagues and administrators to give us adequate support for scholarship, to have generous categories of qualifications and promotion that properly emphasize teaching, and to maintain realistic expectations for hiring, tenure, and promotion. Not every college professor needs to be a great and productive scholar, but every professor must try to become a great and productive teacher. This will happen only when professors are allowed to cultivate and practice the art of teaching unfettered by the disproportionate pressure to publish original research that few people will read. But, you will ask, if college professors don't publish, what will distinguish them from, say, high school teachers?

For starters, an MA or a PhD is an adequate degree to prove their ability to teach at the college level. I'm not talking about these degrees merely as credentials, union cards to teach, but rather as requirements for college-level teaching, even at community colleges, *provided that they set a standard of academic achievement that matches the aims of undergraduate education and prepares graduate students for what they will do at most colleges or universities in the United States today—and that is to teach.* An MA or a PhD should mean that one is competent in one's field *and* qualified to teach—otherwise, we'll continue to hear calls for college professors to be certified like grade school and high school teachers. Should an MA or a PhD be an absolute requirement? No. I don't want a Mandarin system. There's no reason why an accomplished musician, say, like Yo-Yo Ma, shouldn't be allowed to teach in a music department because he doesn't have a PhD. The same should be true for tenure and promotion, but under the current system Yo-Yo Ma would be denied tenure at most colleges and universities because he merely performs and doesn't produce original work. My response is that he has *done something*. He can play music, he can teach others, and he contributes to the aims of liberal education by keeping the tradition of his field alive.

Most college teachers will not have the stature of a Yo-Yo Ma, or be as accomplished, but as a standard of academic achievement, an MA or PhD will show that they have done something too, something above and beyond what high school teachers are expected to do. An MA or a PhD should show that its recipients have mastered a certain level of expertise in both knowledge and skills that qualifies them to teach undergraduate students and critique their work. They must complete sufficient archival research, field work, or lab work, for instance, and demonstrate expertise in the standards of scholarship in their field. They must master a certain level of thought and demonstrate their knowledge and understanding through oral examinations and written work. Written work should become gradually more sophisticated through seminar papers, a master's thesis, and finally a dissertation (or some other capstone project, call it what you will). Although teaching advanced writing, graduate professors should still reinforce the mechanics and elements of good writing that will enable new professors to teach their students as well. None of this requires graduate students to produce groundbreaking or an extraordinarily original work, although some will.

Finally, both MA and PhD students need adequate (and realistic) training as teachers, which most graduate programs do not give them. They should be required to take seminars on the history and philosophy of education in which they read and discuss the classic texts on teaching and learning. This will get them to think about teaching at its theoretical and practical levels early in their careers, and encourage them to develop their own styles and methods of teaching, which they could discuss with other graduate students and professors. They should work with the theater department of their college or university and take courses on speaking and study acting (or join an organization like Toastmasters International). And they should actually teach students, first as an apprentice and then in their own course, a capstone that should be as important as the thesis for receiving the MA or the dissertation for the PhD. By developing these habits in graduate school it is more likely that they will carry them over to their jobs in colleges and universities. Furthermore, in the spirit of collaborative learning (if we force it on our students we might as well practice it ourselves), colleges and universities should set up similar reading groups among faculty to discuss the common books they will teach as part of the great books core and the classic texts on teaching and education, not simply seminars, workshops, and discussion groups in which the resident scholar of teaching and learning peddles the latest wares. This would create a real *academic community* in which professors cultivate teaching and learning together.

I'm not suggesting that genuine scholarship and excellent teaching are exclusive or incompatible. Many genuine scholars are also great undergraduate teachers—my mentor at Syracuse University comes to mind. We forget that for the longest time in France most advanced scholars began by teaching in the *lycée* or *gymnasium*, and in England by teaching in public and grammar schools. Teaching does not preclude genuine scholarship, and if allowed to develop in the way that I have been suggesting throughout this book, it is likely that, given time to ripen and mature, more teachers would become better scholars in time. As the highest form of study, teaching should precede publishing; then scholarship will be more likely to grow out of a professor's teaching; then teaching and scholarship will genuinely inform each other. As things now stand, we have it the other way around.

The third thing we can do save liberal education is to keep a fresh outlook and mind as teachers. "If men are for a long time accustomed only to one sort of method of thoughts," says Locke, "their minds grow stiff in it and do not readily turn to another." Therefore, they should be made to "look into all sorts of knowledge, and exercise their understanding in so wide a variety and stock of knowledge" because it encourages "a variety and freedom of thinking."[3] Rather than spend our summers on small topics suitable for articles we should be thinking about great topics instead. As part of the tenure process, rather than require publications, colleges and universities might require professors to develop at least one new and different course each year. This would encourage professors to think about their subjects in new and various ways, it would ensure that they keep up with the latest research, and it would ensure that teaching remains an intellectual activity. Another suggestion is to allow professors to teach courses on subjects in which they have taken an interest and have begun to cultivate, even if removed from their area of expertise. Or, let them teach Introductory courses from other departments. In the interest of liberal education they should be cultivating universal knowledge anyway.

A fourth thing we can do—and this is certainly within our grasp—is to pay attention to our students, get to know them, and try to understand their needs and concerns. As Allan Bloom writes: "The teacher, particularly the teacher dedicated to liberal education, must constantly try to look toward the goal of human completeness and back at the natures of his students here and now, ever seeking to understand the former and to assess the capacities of the latter to approach it. Attention to the young, knowing what their hungers are and what they can digest, is the essence of the craft. One must spy out and elicit those hungers. For there is no real education that does not respond to felt need; anything else acquired is trifling display."

Finally—and this is also within our grasp—we can return to the classic texts on education and teaching, take from them what is valuable, and develop our own methods and styles of teaching. Those who do will see that these books not only embody a tradition of learning rooted in concrete reality and the world of things, but that they also help us to pose the fundamental questions about education and teaching that we should all be thinking about. They provide us with alternatives to current attitudes and assumptions, and they help us to resist the easy and preferred answers of the scholars of teaching and learning by showing us others worthy of consideration. Above all, those who take them seriously and read them in the spirit in which they were written will discover that teaching is the essence of liberal education itself. As teachers on the front line, we can save liberal education if we strive to become the kinds of educators who will promote its true and proper ends.

NOTES

PREFACE

1. For more on this, see my essay, "Why The Professor Still Can't Teach," *Minding the Campus* (June 17, 2010).
2. A. W. Astin, *What Matters in College?: Four Critical Years Revisited* (San Francisco, CA: Jossey-Bass, 1993), 223.
3. "A Test of Leadership: Charting the Future of U.S. Higher Education (2006). A Report of the Commission Appointed by Secretary of Education Margaret Spellings, at http://www.ed.gov/about/bdscomm/list/hiedfuture/reports/pre-pub-report.pdf; the recent studies by The Center of Inquiry in the Liberal Arts at Wabash College (www.liberalarts.wabash.edu), which cover both small institutions and large universities.
4. The full report, "Writing: A Ticket to Work … Or a Ticket Out, A Survey of Business Leaders," can be read at http://www.writingcommission.org/prod_downloads/writingcom/writing-ticket-to-work.pdf.
5. "What will they learn?: A Report on General Education Requirements at 100 of the Nation's Leading Colleges and Universities" by the American Council of Trustees and Alumni (2009), at https://www.goacta.org/publications/downloads/WhatWillTheyLearnFinal.pdf.
6. For a more detailed critique of the shortcomings of these books, see my review of Mark Taylor's *Crisis on Campus*, "This Is a Bold New Plan For Higher ED?", *Minding the Campus* (October 4, 2010).
7. "Is There Any Knowledge That a Man Must Have?" in *The Knowledge Most Worth Having*, ed., Wayne C. Booth (Chicago, IL: University of Chicago Press, 1967).

CHAPTER 1

1. *The history of Rasselas, prince of Abissinia*, chap. XXX.
2. *The First Year Out: Understanding American Teens after High School* (Chicago, IL: University of Chicago Press, 2007).
3. *The laws of* Plato, trans. Thomas Pangle (Chicago, IL: University of Chicago Press, 1980).
4. *The American University: How It Works, Where It Is Going* (p. 43) (New York, NY: Harper & Row, 1968)
5. The student then felt that it was necessary to add: "Normally I don't go out of my way to praise a teacher, because I am not a big fan of those who come off as brown nosing, but in this case, I make the exception because you're a great teacher in my opinion." I realize that using personal examples might seem self-serving, but I want readers to see that I practice what I preach. I will gladly supply copies of e-mails and course evaluations to anyone who would like proof. I will also supply the names and e-mail addresses of former students who are willing to verify what I write.
6. *Some Thoughts Concerning Education* and *Of the Conduct of the Understanding* Ruth W. Grant and Nathan Tarcov (Eds.). (Indianapolis: Hackett Publishing Co., 1996).
7. Plato, *Symposium*, trans. Kenneth Dover (Cambridge: Cambridge University Press, 1980).
8. Helen Fisher, *Why we love: The nature and chemistry of romantic love* (69) (New York, NY: Henry Holt, 2004); *The neuroscience of adult learning: New directions for adult and continuing education*, S. Johnson & K. Taylor (Eds.) (San Francisco, CA: Jossey-Bass, 2006), "*Key Aspects of How the Brain Learns*" (3–9), James Zull writes: "Emotion is the foundation of learning." In "*Neuroscience and Adult Learning*" (11–19), Louis Cozolino and Susan Sprokay write: "learning is maximized during a moderate state of arousal."
9. My examples come from David A. Sousa, *How the Brain Learns* (3rd ed.) (Thousand Oaks, CA: Corwin Press, 2006) and James E. Zull, *The Art of the Changing Brain* (Sterling, VA: Stylus, 2002); but also see, among other works, Joseph E. LeDoux, *The Emotional Brain* (New York, NY: Simon & Schuster, 1997) and "Emotion, memory, and the brain." In *The Scientific American Book of the Brain* (105–117) (New York, NY: The Lyons Press, 1999); E. T. Rolls, *The Brain and Emotion* (Oxford: Oxford Press, 1999); Pat Wolfe, "The role of meaning and emotion in learning." In *The Neuroscience of Adult Learning: New Directions for Adult and Continuing Education*, (op. cit.), 35–41; Eric Jensen, *Enriching the Brain: How to Maximize Every Learner's Potential* (San Francisco, CA: Jossey-Bass, 2006); and Daniel T. Willingham, *Why Don't Students Like School?: A Cognitive Scientist Answers Questions About How the Mind Works and What It Means for the Classroom* (San Francisco, CA: Jossey-Bass, 2009), chap. 1. I discuss other examples in the next chapter.
10. Cf. Barry G. Scheckley and Sandy Bell, "Experience, consciousness, and learning: Implications for instruction." In *The Neuroscience of Adult Learning*, 43–52; Zull *The Art of the Changing Brain*, chaps. 5 and 7 in general.
11. *Talks to Teachers on Psychology and to Students on Some of Life's Ideals* (Mineoloa, NY: Dover Publications, n.d).

12. *The Aims of Education* (New York, NY: Mentor Books, 1929, 1961), 69.
13. CNN.com, 20 July 2008; http://www.cnn.com/2008/LIVING/07/20/btsc.prison.university/index.html. Cognitive scientist James Zull seems to confirm my suspicion (*The Art of the Changing Brain*, 119–120). For Shorris, see "On the uses of a liberal education II. As a weapon in the hands of the restless poor." *Harper's Magazine*, 259/1768 (September 1997): 50–59; for The Clemente Course, see http://clemente.bard.edu/about.
14. Question XI from *Truth*, trans. Robert W. Mulligan, James V. McGlynn, and Robert William Schmidt (Indianapolis, IN: Hackett Publishing, 1994).
15. Zull, *The Art of the Changing Brain*, 52, 102–105, 122.
16. Ibid., 33; cf. Sousa, *How the Brain Learns*, 40–41; and chaps. 4 and 5.
17. *Novum Organum*, Aphorism CIII.
18. *The Letters of Roger Ascham*, trans. Alvin Vos (New York, NY: Peter Lang Publishing, 1989), 179–185; and Cheke's letter to Edward (1552) In Sir John Harington, *Nugae Antiquae*, 2 Vols. (London, 1804), I. 17–22.
19. *Liberal Education* (New York, NY: Henry Holt and Co., 1943).
20. For more data on student disengagement, see John Pryor, et al., *The American Freshman: Forty Year Trends* (Los Angeles: Higher Education Research Institute, 2007); George D. Kuh, "What student engagement data tell us about college readiness." *Peer Review* 9 (Winter 2007), 6; the 2008 College Senior Survey conducted by the Higher Education Research Institute Graduate School of Education & Information Studies at UCLA (http://www.heri.ucla.edu); and the 2010 study by the Center for Studies in Higher Education at Berkeley (http://cshe.berkeley.edu/publications/docs/SERU_EngagedLearningREPORT_2010.pdf).
21. Gina Barreca, "5 Things professors don't know," *The Chronicle of Higher Education* (16 November 2009) at http://chronicle.com/blogPost/5-Things-Professors-Dont/8867. For additional data on students attitudes, see John Pryor, et al., *The American freshman: Forty year trends* (Los Angeles: Higher Education Research Institute, 2007); George D. Kuh, "What student engagement data tell us about college readiness." *Peer Review* 9 (Winter 2007) 6; the Higher Education Research Institute Graduate School of Education & Information Studies at UCLA (http://www.heri.ucla.edu); and the 2010 study by the Center for Studies in Higher Education at Berkeley (http://cshe.berkeley.edu/publications/docs/SERU_EngagedLearningREPORT_2010.pdf).
22. Zull, *The Art of the Changing Brain*, 52.
23. Once more, modern cognitive scientists reiterate what we already know: "no outside influence or force can cause a brain to learn. It will decide on its own. Thus, one important rule for helping people to learn is *to help the learner feel she is in control*. This is probably the best trick that good teachers have" (Zull, *The Art of the Changing Brain*, 52; see chap. 12 as well).

CHAPTER 2

1. *Real Education: Four Simple Rules for Bringing America's Schools Back to Reality* (Crown Forum, 2008), chap. 3.
2. *Why Don't Students Like School?*, chap. 1.

3. Book II, chap. XIV, §13.
4. Dante, *Paradise*, Canto V, 40–42; Emerson, "Memory;" Van Doren, *Liberal Education*, 94–96. On the value of rote learning, see Mihaly Csikszentmihalyi, *Flow: The psychology of optimal experience* (New York, NY: Harper Perennial Modern Classics, 1990), 123–124; H. E Carrett, *Great Experiments in Psychology* (Boston, 1941); P. Suppies, *The Impact of Research on Education* (Washington, D.C., 1978). Cf. Willingham, *Why Don't Students Like School?* and Sousa, *How the Brain Learns*, 86–88; in general, chap. 3. As if he were making my point for me, Sousa points out that the "concept of rehearsal is not new. Even the Greek scholars of 400 BC knew its value. They wrote: *Repeat again what you hear; for by often hearing and saying the same things, what you have learned comes complete into your memory*" (citing the Dialexeis).
5. My sample includes: *How People Learn: Brain, Mind, Experience, and School* Eds., John D. Bransford, Ann L. Brown, and Rodney R. Cocking (Washington, D.C: National Academy Press, 1999), available on line at http://www.nap.edu/html/howpeople1; James E. Zull, *The Art of the Changing Brain* (op. cit.) and "Key aspects of how the brain learns." In *The Neuroscience of Adult Learning*, 3–9; David A. Sousa, *How the Brain Learns*, 3rd ed. (Corwin Press, 2006); Eric Jensen, *Enriching the Brain: How to Maximize Every Learner's Potential* (San Francisco, CA: Jossey-Bass, 2006); and Daniel T. Willingham, *Why Don't Students Like School? A Cognitive Scientist Answers Questions About How the Mind Works and What It Means for the Classroom* (Jossey-Bass, 2009); and various essays by cognitive scientists compiled in *The Scientific American Book of the Brain* (New York, NY: The Lyons Press, 1999), esp. Parts III and VI.
6. Eric R. Kandel and Robert D. Hawkins, "The Biological Basis of Learning and Individuality." *Scientific American Book of the Brain*, 139–154.
7. Patricia S. Goldman-Rakic, "Working Memory and the Mind," in ibid., 91–104, at 92.
8. *Why Don't Students Like School?*, 11–12.
9. Francis Crick and Christof Koch, "The problem of consciousness." *Scientific American Book of the Brain*, 311–323, at 315. Cf. Barry G. Scheckley and Sandy Bell, "Experience, consciousness, and learning: Implications for instruction," In *The Neuroscience of Adult Learning*, pp. 43–52. For an accessible introduction to the topic, see Gerald M. Edelman, *Wider Than the Sky: The Phenomenal Gift of Consciousness* (New Haven, CT: Yale University Press, 2004).
10. Joseph E. LeDoux, "Emotion, Memory, and the Brain." In *Scientific American Book of the Brain*, 105–117.
11. Cozolino and Sprokay, "*Neuroscience and adult learning.*" 13.
12. In addition to Lieber's book and the books by cognitive scientists cited in note 5 above, see these other currently popular books on the market Maryellen Weimer, *Learner-centered teaching: Five key changes to practice* (San Francisco, CA: Jossey-Bass, 2002); L. Dee Fink, *Creating Significant Learning Experiences* (San Francisco, CA: Jossey-Bass, 2003); Robert B. Barr and John Tagg, "From teaching to learning: A new paradigm for undergraduate education." *Change* (November/December 1995); James M. Banner, Jr. and Harold C. Cannon, *The Elements of Teaching* (New Haven, CT: Yale University Press,

1997), Ken Bain, *What the Best College Teachers Do* (Cambridge, MA: Harvard University Press, 2004); and James Lang, *On Course: A Week-by-Week Guide to Your First Semester of College* (Harvard University Press, 2008). The books and articles are too many to catalogue here.
13. Carl Wieman, "Why not try a scientific approach to scientific education." *Change* (September/October 2007): 9–15.
14. *The Art of the Changing Brain*, 59–63.
15. *The Neuroscience of Adult Learning*, 7–8; 1; 35.
16. *Flow: The Psychology of Optimal Experience* (New York, NY: Harper & Row, 1990), chaps. 2 and 3, cf. Arum and Roksa, *Academically Adrift* (93 ff.), who cite numerous studies showing that "when faculty have high expectations, students learn more."
17. *The house of intellect* (New York, NY: Harper & Row, 1959).
18. Cf. Sousa, *How the Brain Learns*, 142–145.
19. I first learned about this theory in Gilbert Highet's *The Art of Teaching* (Vintage Books, 1989). This indispensible text was first published in 1950.
20. "On the uses of a liberal education I. As lite entertainment for bored college students." *Harper's Magazine* 259/1768 (September 1997), 39–49.
21. *What Matters in College: Four Critical Years Revisited* (Jossey-Bass, 1993), 398; Richard Arum and Josia Roksa, *Academically Adrift: Limited Learning on College Campuses* (Chicago, 2011), 100–102. They also write: "There is a positive association between learning time spent studying alone, but a negative association between learning and time spent studying with peers. Thus, the more time students spend studying alone, the more they improve their CLA [College Learning Assessment] performance. In contrast, the more time students spend studying with peers, the smaller their improvement on the CLA." They conclude that group work and collaborative learning have not lived up to the hype.
22. Zull, *The Art of the Changing Brain*, 122; *Why Don't Students Like School?*, 63.

CHAPTER 3

1. These are taken from Harold Laski, "Teacher and Student," In *The Dangers of Obedience and Other Essays* (New York, NY: Harper and Brothers, 1930), 91–120.
2. Clifford Orwin, "Remembering Allan Bloom," *The American Scholar* 62/3 (Summer 1993), 423–430 at 424.
3. "Of the education of children," In *The Complete Essays of Montaigne*, trans. Donald Frame (Stanford: Stanford University Press, 1958).
4. Howard Fine, "What Caused Bobby Jindal's Speech to Be a Disaster?" The Huffington Post (February 26, 2009), at http://www.huffingtonpost.com/howard-fine/what-caused-bobby-jindals_b_170179.html. Fine is the founder of Howard Fine Acting Studio (http://www.howardfine.com).
5. Three standard works of classical rhetoric are Aristotle's *Rhetoric*, Cicero's *De Oratore*, and Quintilian's *Institutio oratoria*. Two useful modern books of rhetoric are: Mortimer J. Adler, *How to Speak, How to Listen* (New York,

NY: Touchstone, 1997) and Wayne C. Booth, *The Rhetoric of RHETORIC: The Quest for Effective Communication* (Wiley-Blackwell, 2004).
6. Recent studies confirm the connection between teacher enthusiasm and student learning. The passions that teachers display for their subject play a central role "in holding students' attention, generating student interest, and developing students' positive attitudes toward learning." See Robert T. Tauber and Cathy Sargent Mester, *Acting Lessons for Teachers: Using Performance Skills in the Classroom* (Westport, CT: Praeger Publishers, 1994). And according to cognitive scientist Louis Cozolino, a "*safe and empathetic relationship* establishes an emotional and neurobiological context conducive to the work of neural reorganization. It serves as a buffer and scaffolding within which [the student] can better tolerate the stress required for neural recognition" (*The Neuroscience of Psychotherapy: Building and Rebuilding the Human Brain* [Norton, 2002], 291, author's italics).
7. *Phaedrus*, 277b-c in Plato, *Complete Works*, ed. John M. Cooper (Indianapolis, IN: Hackett Publishing, 1997).
8. John Henry Newman, *The Rise and Progress of Universities* in *Historical Sketches* (London: Longman, Green, 1909), 9.
9. Daniel T. Willingham, "The Privileged Status of Story," *American Educator* (Summer 2004) and *Why Don't Students Like School?*, chap. 3; Jeremy Hsu, "The Secrets Of Storytelling: Why We Love A Good Yarn," *Scientific American Mind* (September 18, 2008); Zull, *The Art of the Changing Brain*, 229; Louis Cozolino and Susan Sprokay, "Key Aspects of How the Brain Learns," In *The Neuroscience of Adult Learning: New Directions for Adult and Continuing Education*, eds. Sandra Johnson and Kathleen Taylor (San Francisco, CA: Jossey-Bass 2006), 11–19 at 16–17.
10. Mark Edmundson, "On the Uses of a Liberal Education I. As Lite Entertainment for Bored College Students," *Harper's Magazine* 259/1768 (September 1997): 39–49.
11. B. Rammell, "The Poetic Experience of Surprise and the Art of Teaching," *The English Journal* 67/5 (1978): 22–25.
12. Jacques Barzun, "What Is teaching?," *The Atlantic Monthly* (December 1944), 81–87.
13. M. D. Baughman, "Teaching with Humor: A Performing Art," *Contemporary Education* 51/1(1979): 26–30; R. W. Hanning, "The Classroom as Theater of Self: Some Observations for Beginning Teachers," *ADE Bulletin* 77 (1984): 33–37.
14. James, *Talks to Teachers*, 55.
15. Cf. Highet, *The Art of Teaching*. This is one reason why online courses or simply videotaping lectures and putting them online is an insufficient means of instruction.
16. G. K. Chesterton, *The Man Who Was Thursday* (New York, NY: Dodd, Mead, 1908), chap. 3
17. Cicely Berry, *Voice and the Actor* (Wiley Publishing, 1973). Another modern classic text on the subject worth consulting is Virgil Anderson's *Training the Speaking Voice*, 3rd ed. (Oxford: Oxford University Press, 1977). The

connection between acting and speaking is covered Quintilian, *Institutio oratoria*, Book I, chap XI; for delivery, see Book XI, chap. III.
18. St. Augustine, *Concerning the Teacher*, trans. G. C. Leckie In *Basic Writing of St. Augustine*, vol. 1, ed. Whitney J. Oates (New York, NY: Random House, 1948), 395.
19. From the essay "Of Democritus and Heraclitus." Chekov, *To the Actor on techniques of acting* (London: Routledge, 2002). Also worth consulting is Viola Spolin's *Improvisation for the Theater: A Handbook of Teaching and Directing Techniques*, 3rd ed. (Northwestern University Press, 1999). Again, however, all this has been covered by Quintilian.
20. Quintilian writes: "for the best expressions are such as are least far-fetched, and have an air of simplicity, appearing to spring from truth itself. Those which betray care, refuse to appear otherwise than artificial and studied; they fail to exhibit grace, and do not produce conviction; besides that, they observe the sense, and choke the crop as it were, with a superabundance of herbage" (Book VIII, Introduction).
21. Chekov, *To the Actor*, 3.
22. In "Effective Lecturing Techniques," *The Clearing House* 55 (1981), 20–23, Richard Weaver writes: "The real problem with college teaching is that so few college professors are passionate about teaching. Most approach teaching as a job or a distraction which inhibits them from generating the enthusiasm that will enable them to teach well."
23. Quoted in Alison Lurie, *The Language of Clothes* (New York, NY: Random House, 1981), on whom I rely for what follows.
24. *The Importance of Wearing Clothes* (Los Angeles: Elysium Growth Press, 1991). This book was first published in 1959.
25. Jacques Barzun, *The House of Intellect* (New York, NY: Harper & Brothers, 1959), 113–114.

CHAPTER 4

1. Bok, *Our Underachieving Colleges*, 116–117, see his references on these pages for the data.
2. John Comenius, *The Great Didactic*, trans. M. W. Keating, 2 vols. (A+C Black, LTD, 1923).
3. Montaigne, "Of the art of discussion"; cf. Quintilian, *Institutio oratoria*, Book V, chaps. XXVIII–XXIX.
4. *The Art of Cross-Examination* (New York, NY: Collier Books, 1962), 28; 36 for the quotes below.
5. As a classicist, he would know better than most. For what follows, I have benefited tremendously from chap. 3, In *The Art of Teaching*.
6. Cf. Sandra Johnson, "The Neuroscience of the Mentor-Learner Relationship," in *The Neuroscience of Adult Learning*, 63–69.
7. *Republic*, 511a–d. A hypothesis is literally "a placing under," but can also be called a "supposition." And you may substitute Plato's use of the word

"beginning" with "starting-point," or "principle," or "cause." Similarly, you may substitute Plato's use of "end" with "conclusion" or "result." Whatever words you choose, this is the essence of argument and understanding. See notes 36–38 to this book in the Bloom translation for the explanation of the various uses of these words.

8. Cf. Sandra Johnson, "The Neuroscience of the Mentor-Learner Relationship," In *The Neuroscience of Adult Learning: New Directions for Adult and Continuing Education*, eds. Sandra Johnson and Kathleen Taylor (San Francisco, CA: Jossey-Bass 2006), 35–41.

9. *Flow: The psychology of optimal experience* (New York, NY: Harper Perennial Modern Classics, 1990); and James P. Carse, *Breakfast at the Victory: The Mysticism of Ordinary Experience* (New York, NY: Harper-Collins, 1994), 68070, for what follows.

10. Cognitive scientist James Zull makes the same point (*The Art of the Changing Brain*, 60): "If we learn how to get our students more involved in their work, they will feel *less* nervous and afraid. If we focus on the work itself rather than the extrinsic reward, the intrinsic reward systems can begin to engage." Cf. Sandra Johnson, "The Neuroscience of the Mentor-Learner Relationship," In *The Neuroscience of Adult Learning*, 66: Dialogue "creates the holding environment that assists the learner in moving his or her emotions" to the higher regions of the brain, prompting it to release "pleasure chemicals" that "produce a reward that motivates the learner to continue to move along this developmental path."

11. Plutarch, *Moralia* I, trans. Frank Cole Babbit (Cambridge, MA: Loeb Classical Library). Also see the second half of *How to Speak, How to Listen*; and the illuminating essay by Daniel M. Gross, "The Art of Listening: A Course in the Humanities," *International Journal of Listening* 21/1 (April 2007): 72–79.

12. Stephen D. Brookfield and Stephen Preskill, *Discussion as a Way of Teaching: Tools and Techniques for Democratic Classrooms*, 2nd ed. (San Francisco, CA: Jossey-Bass, 1999), 44–48.

13. The study is by Ambient Insight (http://www.ambientinsight.com/Reports/eLearning.aspx); cf. David Nagel, "Most College Students To Take Classes Online by 2014," *Campus Technology* (October 28, 2009) at http://campus-technology.com/articles/2009/10/28/most-college-students-to-take-classes-online-by-2014.aspx; "Virtual ivy: why the US needs more e-colleges," *The Christian Science Monitor* (August 31, 2009) at http://www.csmonitor.com/2009/0831/p08s01-comv.html; Barack Obama, "Rebuilding Something Better," *The Washington Post* (July 12, 2009), at http://www.washingtonpost.com/wp-dyn/content/article/2009/07/11/AR2009071100647.html.

14. Kevin Carey, "College for $99 a Month," *Washington Monthly* (September/October 2009) at http://www.washingtonmonthly.com/college_guide/feature/college_for_99_a_month.php; for the students' comments, see "Getting An Education On The Internet," NPR: Talk of the Nation (September 22, 2009) at http://www.npr.org/templates/story/story.php?storyId=113073691; on the rising cost of higher education, see CNNMoney.com, "College: More expensive than ever" (October 20, 2009) at http://money.cnn.com/2009/10/19/pf/college_costs/index.htm?postversion=2009102013. For other compelling reasons for

online instruction, see William Pannapacker, "Online Learning: Reaching Out to the Skeptics" (*The Chronicle of Higher* education, September 18, 2009) at http://chronicle.com/article/Online-Learning-Reaching-Out/48375.

15. Linda F. Cornelious and Yi Yang, "Preparing Instructors for Quality Online Instruction," Online Journal of Distance Learning Administration, Volume VIII, Number I, Spring 2005, at http://www.westga.edu/~distance/ojdla/spring81/yang81.htm.

16. *Our Underachieving Colleges*, 116–118; cf. David W. Johnson, Roger T. Johnson, and Karl A. Smith, *Cooperative Learning: Increasing College Faculty Instructional Productivity* (San Francisco, CA: Jossey-Bass, 1991), 6–8. Two recent reports, sponsored by the Community College Research Center, show that community college students in online classes performed worse than those in face-to-face classes. See Di Xu & Shanna Smith Jaggars, "Online and Hybrid Course Enrollment and Performance in Washington State Community and Technical Colleges" (CCRC Working Paper No. 31, March 2011) at http://ccrc.tc.columbia.edu/Publication.asp?UID=872 and Shanna Smith Jaggars & Di Xu, "Online Learning in the Virginia Community College System" (September 2010) at http://ccrc.tc.columbia.edu/Publication.asp?uid=813.

17. Louis Cozolino and Susan Sprokay, "Neuroscience and Adult Learning," In *The Neuroscience of Adult Learning*, 12–13.

18. John T. Cacioppo and William Patrick, *Loneliness: Human Nature and the Need for Social Connection* (New York, NY: W. W. Norton, 2008); Michael J. Bugeja, *Interpersonal Divide: The Search for Community in a Technological Age* (Oxford: Oxford University Press, 2005). Also see Johannah Cornblatt, "Lonely Planet: Despite our inter-connectedness, we're now more alone than ever," *Newsweek Web Exclusive* (August 21, 2009) at http://www.newsweek.com/id/213088.

19. "Evaluation of Evidence-Based Practices in Online Learning: A Meta-Analysis and Review of Online Learning Studies," at http://www.ed.gov/rschstat/eval/tech/evidence-based-practices/finalreport.pdf. For modern student outcome I'll refer the reader back to the preface of this book.

20. See Csikszentmihalyi, *Flow*, 28, 31, 58; Eyal Ophira, Clifford Nassb, Anthony D. Wagnerc, "Cognitive control in media multitaskers," *Proceedings of the National Academy of Science, Vol. 106 No. 33 (August 2009);* and Christine Rosen, "The Myth of Multitasking," *The New Atlantis: A Journal of Technology & Society* 20 (2008): 105–110 at www.TheNewAtlantis.com. This is a good summary of latest research on the disadvantages of multitasking, especially when it comes to learning. The following quotation is taken from this article.

21. Cf. Bauerlein, *The Dumbest Generation*; see chaps. 3–4 for the impact of visual media and technology on learning. Colleges and universities are struggling to accommodate student use of Bandwidth, which is increasingly being used, not for research purposes, but for peer to peer (P2P) file sharing. In fact, this accounts for 22% of total bandwidth used on campuses. Dian Schaffhauser, "Bandwidth Battle: How Entertainment is Strangling Education on Higher Ed Networks," *Campus Technology* (November 13, 2009) at http://campustechnology.com/articles/2009/11/13/bandwidth-battle-how-entertainment-is-strangling-education-on-higher-ed-networks.aspx.

CHAPTER 5

1. The statistic is also reported on Justice O'Connor's web site, Our Courts (http://www.ourcourts.org/about-our-courts), which she initiated to promote civic education. She appeared on "The Daily Show with Jon Stewart" on March 3, 2009. The interview can be viewed on the Daily Show's web site (www.thedailyshow.com). Similarly, a recent Marist Poll (July 1, 2011) showed that only 58% of Americans knew that the United States declared its independence in 1776; 26% were unsure; and 16% mentioned another date. While 1 in 4 Americans didn't know that the United States declared independence from Great Britain. (See http://maristpoll.marist.edu/71-independence-day-dummy-seventeen-seventy-when.)
2. See the Associated Press-Ipsos poll released in August 2007, from which the Bustos quotation is taken. According to the National Endowment of the Arts, the percentage of Americans who read any book not required for work fell from 56.6% in 2002 to 54.3% in 2008. See "More Americans Are Reading, but..." Publishers Weekly (January 19, 2009), at http://www.publishersweekly.com/pw/print/20090119/2247-more-americans-are-reading-but--html. For the NEA study, "Follow-up to Reading at Risk links declines in reading with poorer academic and social outcomes" (November 19, 2007) at http://www.nea.gov/news/news07/TRNR.html; cf. A Test of Leadership: Charting the Future of U.S. Higher Education (2006). A Report of the Commission Appointed by Secretary of Education Margaret Spellings, at http://www.ed.gov/about/bdscomm/list/hiedfuture/reports/pre-pub-report.pdf. Also see the studies by the National Assessment of Adult Literacy (at http://nces.ed.gov/naal/), Bauerlein, *The Dumbest Generation*, chap. 2, and Arum and Roksa's *Academically Adrift*, chap. 4.
3. Mortimer J. Adler and Charles Van Doren, *How to Read a Book* (New York, NY: Touchstone, 1972), 8. The first edition, published in 1940, is a much better read, in my opinion, and still worth consulting. In this chapter, I also rely on Jacques Barzun, "Of What Use the Classics Today," In *Begin Here: The Forgotten Conditions of Teaching and Learning* (Chicago, IL: University of Chicago Press, 1991), chap. 10 and *Teacher in America* (Indianapolis, IN: Liberty Fund, 1981), chap. 11. Barzun's influence on my views will be evident throughout. I have adapted his criteria of a great book from *Begin Here*, 133–135. All quotations from Thoreau are from his chapter on Reading in *Walden*.
4. Not that people have not tried to identify a canon. See, for example, Harold Bloom, *The Western Canon: The Books and School of the Ages* (New York, NY: Harcourt Brace, 1994).
5. The letter is printed in *The Prince*, trans. Harvey Mansfield, 2nd ed. (Chicago, IL: University of Chicago Press, 1998), 107–111.
6. Trans. Allan Bloom.
7. Jean-Jacques Rousseau, *Emile, or On Education*, trans. Allan Bloom (New York, NY: Basic Books, 1979).
8. *Liberal Education*, 95.
9. Not surprisingly, the most vocal defenders of textbooks tend to be their authors. See, for example, Robert Brooker, "The Value of a Textbook,"

Inside Higher Education (June 2, 2008). Most of the comments responding to this article reinforce my point. For more on the textbook racket, see Chris Anderson, *The Long Tail: Why the Future of Business Is Selling Less of More* (New York, NY: Hyperion, 2006), 86–87 ff.
10. Bok, *Our Underachieving Colleges*, 121; cf. Grant Wiggins, *Educative Assessment: Designing Assessments to Inform and Improve Student Performance* (San Francisco, CA: Jossey-Bass, 1998).
11. Francis Bacon, "Advice to Fulke Greville on his studies," In *A Critical Edition of the Major Works*, ed. Brian Vickers (Oxford: Oxford University Press, n.d.).
12. Sousa, *How The Brain Learns*, 138, 141, 247.
13. Jensen, *Enriching the Brain*, 76–78; cf. Sousa, *How the Brain Learns*, 50.
14. *Mathematics for Nonmathematicians* (Mineola, NY: Dover Publications, 1967). Like William James, Kline believed that mathematics is part of the humanities and as such should be taught historically within the liberal arts curriculum. One should also see his *Mathematics in Western Culture* (Oxford: Oxford University Press, 1964).
15. For these and the following points, as well as a detailed discussion of the cumulative effect of reading, see Bauerlein, *The Dumbest Generation*, 58–59 in particular, chap. 2 in general. Also see, Mark Edmundson, *Why Read?* (Bloomsbury USA, 2004).
16. Zull, *The Art of the Changing Brain*, 42.
17. Jensen, *Enriching the Brain*, 67–68, 77–78, 180–182 (and his references).
18. Eric R. Kandel and Robert D. Hawkins, "The Biological Basis of Learning and Individuality," In *The Scientific America Book of the Brain*, 139–154, at 140; cf. Sousa, *How The Brain Learns*, 84: "Students are much more likely to remember curriculum content in which they have made an emotional investment. For this to happen, teachers often need to use strategies that get students emotionally involved with the learning content."
19. I owe these references and quotations to Bauerlein, *The Dumbest Generation*, 56–57.
20. Jensen, *Enriching the Brain*, 69–70 (and his references). Jensen writes that researchers "found that learners who had more challenge and more complexity in their academic schedules had more dendritic growth and connectivity." For the college-age learners of one study, "the greater the complexity in their lives, the greater the complexity that was found in their brains."
21. *The Aims of Education*, 68.
22. *The Closing of the American Mind* (New York, NY: Simon & Schuster, 1997).

CHAPTER 6

1. I realize my assumption may be faulty, but any student who cannot read at this level should not be in college.
2. *Of the Conduct of the Understanding*, eds., Ruth W. Grant and Nathan Tarcov (Indianapolis, IN: Hackett Publishing Co., 1996), § 20.
3. For those who are skeptical that this is possible, see William James, "How Two Minds Can Know One Thing" (March, 1905); also see Sandra Johnson,

"The Neuroscience of the Mentor-Learner Relationship," In *The Neuroscience of Adult Learning*, 66; and L. Daloz, *Mentor: Guiding the Journey of Adult Learners* (San Francisco, CA: Jossey-Bass, 1986), 226.
4. For what follows, I rely on Allan Bloom, "The Study of Texts," In *Giants and Dwarfs: Essays 1960–1990* (New York, NY: Simon & Schuster, 1990), 295–314, and his illuminating Foreword to *Emile* and Preface to *The Republic*.
5. *Of the Conduct of the Understanding*, § 20.
6. See Adler, *How to Read A Book*, chap. 20.
7. See my article in the journal *Quidditas* 29 (2008), for a detailed description of my approach in a course I have taught called, "Love from the Twelfth to the Twentieth Centuries," using Denis de Rougement's *Love in the Western World*, rev. ed. (New Jersey: Princeton University Press, 1983). The article is available online: http://humanities.byu.edu/rmmra/pdfs/29.pdf.
8. Sousa, *How The Brain Learns*, 50.
9. Arthur Schopenhauer, "On Books and Reading," In *Essays*, trans. T. Bailey Saunders (A. L. Burt Co., n.d.).
10. *Liberal Education*, 101.
11. Sousa, *How The Brain Learns*, 247. Of course, Montaigne already warned us against this presumption of progress in the sixteenth century: Anyone "intoxicated with his knowledge when he looks beneath him" ought first to look "upward toward past ages;" then he will "lower his horns, finding there so many thousands of minds that trample him underfoot."
12. Barzun, *Begin Here*, 35.
13. A. W. Astin, *What Matters in College: Four Critical Years Revisited* (San Francisco, CA: Jossey-Bass, 1993), 334, 425; Bok, *Our Underachieving Colleges*, 273; David A. Sousa, *How The Brain Learns*, 3rd ed. (Thousand Oaks, CA: Corwin Press, 2006), 138, 141, 247; Eric Jensen, *Enriching the Brain: How To Maximize Every Learner's Potential* (San Francisco, CA: Jossey-Bass, 2006), 34–35.
14. Jensen, *Enriching the Brain*, 77–78, 12; cf. B. Jacobs, M. Schall, and A. Schiebel, "A Quantitative Dendritic Analysis of Bernice's Area in Humans. II. Gender, Hemispsheric and Environmental Factors," *The Journal of Comparative Neurology* 327 (1993): 97–111.
15. *Real Education*, 115–116, for what follows in this paragraph. In general, see chaps. 3 and 4. Also see, Anne E. Cunningham and Keith E. Stanovich, "What Reading Does for the Mind," *American Educator* (Spring/Summer 1998): 1–8.
16. See the Wabash National Study of Liberal Arts conducted by the Center of Inquiry in the Liberal Arts at Wabash College (www.liberalarts.wabash.edu). The criteria included: (1) academic challenge and effort; (2) frequency of higher-order exams and assignments; (3) challenging classes and high faculty expectations; (4) integrating ideas, information, and experiences. Also see the statistics mentioned in my Preface.
17. For elaboration on this point, see my "Students Adrift? Don't Blame Them," *Minding the Campus* (January 31, 2011).
18. *Of the Conduct of the Understanding*, § 12.

CHAPTER 7

1. For another defense of this kind of academic writing, see *Just Being Difficult? Academic Writing in the Public Arena*, eds., Jonathan Culler and Kevin Lamb (Stanford, CA: Stanford University Press, 2003) and Mark Bauerlein's review, "Bad Writing's Back," *Philosophy and Literature* 28 (2004): 180–191.
2. The books to consult are: William Strunk, Jr., *The Elements of Style* (Mineoloa, NY: Dover Publications, 2006); Sir Ernest Gowers, *The Complete Plain Words*, revised by Sidney Greenbaum and Janet Whitcut, 3rd ed. (London: Penguin Books 1986); William K. Zinsser, *On Writing Well, 25th Anniversary: The Classic Guide to Writing Nonfiction* (New York, NY: Collins, 2001); Jack Lynch, *The English Language: A User's Guide* (Newburyport, MA: Focus Publishing, 2008). One should also consult Jacques Barzun, *Simple and Direct: A Rhetoric for Writers* (Chicago, IL: Chicago University Press, 1985). These should be required reading for *all* teachers and students. I have begun requiring students to purchase Strunk and Lynch's books.
3. *Essay Concerning Human Understanding*, III.11. The entire chapter should be read.
4. See Chap. 3, esp. pp. 21–22 where he provides a useful synopsis of the elements of good writing. I photocopy and hand it out to my students.
5. See for example, Netlingo.com. By the way, the sentence translates, "Oh my God, adults are in the room, I'll talk to you later."
6. *BAD or, The Dumbing of America* (New York, NY: Touchstone, 1991).
7. "Of physiognomy," In *The Complete Essays of Montaigne* (*op. cit.*).
8. For example, see the Report of the National Commission on Writing (May 2006) at http://www.writingcommission.org/prod_downloads/writing-com/writing-school-reform-natl-comm-writing.pdf.
9. Bok, *Our Underachieving Colleges*, 89, 91. For what follows in the next paragraph see pp. 83–91 specifically, but chap. 4 in general; and see Astin, *What Matters in College*, 223.
10. College professors are not the only ones facing this problem, according to the National Commission on Writing (2003 study): "While the task of teaching writing has to be shoehorned into the time available during the day, the sheer number of students facing the elementary teacher is not an insuperable obstacle to teaching writing. Many upper-level teachers, on the other hand, face between 120 and 200 students, weekly if not daily. Teachers of English (or history or biology) who ask simply for a weekly 1-page paper are immediately overwhelmed with the challenge of reading, responding to, and evaluating what their request produces" (p. 58).
11. See for example, Peter Smagorinsky, "Is It Time to Abandon the Idea of 'Best Practices' in the Teaching of English?," *English Journal* 98/6 (2009): 12–22; and George Hillocks Jr., "Some Practices and Approaches Are Clearly Better Than Others and We Had Better Not Ignore the Differences," *English Journal* 98/6 (2009): 23–29. Cf. Thomas Bartlett, "Why Johnny Can't Write, Even Though He Went to Princeton, "*The Chronicle of Higher Education* (3 January 2003)

at https://chronicle.com/article/Why-Johnny-Cant-Write-Even/35918; and Stanley Fish, "Keep Your Eye on the Small Picture," *The Chronicle of Higher Education* (February 1, 2002), at http://chronicle.com/article/Keep-Your-Eye-on-the-Small/46229; Joseph Smigelski, "Why Can't Tiffany Write?", *The Huffington Post* (June 1, 2010) at http://www.huffingtonpost.com/joseph-smigelski/why-cant-tiffany-write_b_590191.htm.

12. Smagorinsky, "Is It Time to Abandon the Idea of 'Best Practices' in the Teaching of English?," 18.
13. *The King's English: A Guide to Modern Usage* (New York, NY: St. Martin Griffin, 1997), 11.
14. *Practicing History: Selected Essays* (New York, NY: Ballantine Books, 1981).
15. Zull, "Key Aspects of How the Brain Learns," In *The Neuroscience of Adult Learning*, 5.
16. *The Summing Up* (1938), XIII.
17. *Simple and Direct*, 199–200. I have condensed and modified his questions.
18. The study also recommended that "Colleges and universities have an obligation to improve teacher preparation (discussed under Recommendation 5) and make writing more central to their own programs of study. The teaching of writing at the college level should be infused across the curriculum. Formal courses in the teaching of writing (including English Composition) should be the responsibility of well-trained, qualified professional staff." The 2003 Report of the National Commission on Writing in the May 2006 Report at http://www.writingcommission.org/prod_downloads/writingcom/writing-school-reform-natl-comm-writing.pdf.
19. See for example, a recent edition of *Advocate* 26/6 (June 2009), published by the *National Education Association* (www.nea.org). The appropriate section is *Thriving in Academe* (pp. 5–8), of which the leading question is, "Too Much Time Grading Papers?"
20. On multiple-choice exams, Banesh Hoffman's *The Tyranny of Testing* (1962) is still worth reading. Hoffman shows how they work against everything higher education aims to promote: The natural diversity of minds, the production of imaginative students, and the questioning of conventional opinions. They produce what I call "Jeopardy learning," or the ability to spit out facts, at which the mediocre and second-best students usually excel. Cf. Zull, *The Art of the Changing Brain*, Chaps. 1 and 7.

CHAPTER 8

1. See for example, Anya Kamenetz's essay, "Wanted: Really Smart Suckers," *The Village Voice*, April 20, 2004, at http://www.villagevoice.com/2004-04-20/news/wanted-really-smart-suckers; and her most recent book, *DIY U: Edupunks, Edupreneurs, and the Coming Transformation of Higher Education* (White River Jct., Vermont: Chelsea Green Publishing, 2010). Also, see William Pannapacker

(AKA Thomas Benton), "Graduate School in the Humanities: Just Don't Go" (January 30, 2009); "Just Don't Go, Part 2" (March 13, 2009); and "The Big Lie About the 'Life of the Mind,'" (February 8, 2009).
2. "The Disadvantages of an Elite Education," *American Scholar* (Summer 2008).
3. Locke, *Of the Conduct of the Understanding*, § 19. A point also made by Quintilian, *Institutio oratoria*, Book I, chap. XII, 2–7.

SUGGESTED READINGS

The following books are intended to serve as an introduction to the history and philosophy of education. They are only suggestions. They are not exclusive or the only books on the subject that can or should be read. Readers will accept or reject or modify this list, and they should, because ultimately what we value and find useful is that which we make our own. Readers with limited time may wish to start with the books marked with asterisks.

Adler, M. J. (1997). *How to speak, how to listen*. New York, NY: Touchstone.
*Adler, M. J. & van Doren C. (1972). *How to read a book*. New York, NY: Touchstone. The first edition, published in 1940, is still worth consulting.
*Aquinas, T. (1994). Questions X and XI in *Truth*, trans. R. W. Mulligan, J. V. McGlynn & R. W. Schmidt. Indianapolis, IN: Hackett Publishing.
Aristotle (1984). *The Complete Works: The Revised Oxford Translation*, Ed., Jonathan Barnes, 2 vols. Princeton, NJ: Princeton University Press.
 See especially *Rhetoric, nicomachean ethics, politics, poetics, metaphysics*, and his six works on logic (known collectively as the Organon in the Middle Ages). Cf. William Kneale and Martha Kneale, *The development of logic*. Oxford: Oxford University Press. 1962, 1984.
Ascham, R. (1967) *The scholemaster* (1570). Menston, England: The Scolar Press Limited.
Augustine (1995). *Against the academicians and the teacher*, trans. P. King. Indianapolis, IN: Hackett Publishing.
Bacon, F. (n.d.), *A critical edition of the major works*, Ed.. B. Vickers Oxford: Oxford University Press.
See the letters "Advice to the Earl of Rutland on his travels" and "Advice to Fulke Greville on his studies"; the essay "Of studies"; and *The advancement of learning*.
*Barzun, J. (1991). *Begin Here: The Forgotten Conditions of Teaching and Learning*. Chicago, IL, The University of Chicago Press; *Teacher in America* (Liberty Fund, 1981), first published in 1945; *Simple and direct: A rhetoric for writers*

130 SUGGESTED READINGS

(Chicago, IL, The University of Chicago Press, 1985); *The house of intellect* (New York, NY: Harper & Row, 1959). In general, I recommend anything written by Barzun.

Bloom, A. (1997). *The closing of the American mind*. New York, NY: Simon & Schuster.

Bloom, A. (1990) "The Study of Texts," In *Giants and dwarfs: Essays 1960–1990* (pp. 295–314). New York, NY: Simon and Schuster

Chesterfield, L. (1992). *Letters*. Oxford: Oxford University Press.

Cicero (1942). *De Oratore*, trans. E. W. Sutton, 2 vols. Cambridge, MA: Loeb Classical Library.

Csikszentmihalyi, M. (1990). *Flow: The psychology of optimal experience*. (New York, NY: Harper & Row.

Comenius, J. (1923). *The great didactic*, trans. M. W. Keating, 2 vols. (A+C Black, LTD).

de Tocqueville, A. (2000). *Democracy in America*, trans. H. C. Mansfield & D. Winthrop. Chicago, IL: The University of Chicago Press. The relevant readings can be found in Vol. 2, Parts I and II.

Dewey, J. (1964). *On education: Selected writings*. Ed., R. D. Archambault. Chicago, IL: University of Chicago Press. Also see *How We Think* (Mineoloa, NY: Dover Publications, 1999).

Eliot, T. S. (1932). "Modern education and the classics." In *Selected essays* (3rd ed.) (pp. 507–516). London: Faber, 1951.

Eliot, T. S. (1944). "What is a classic?" In *On poetry and poets* (pp. 53–71). London: Faber, 1956.

Elyot, T. (1992). *The boke named the governour*, Ed., D. W. Rude. New York, NY: Garland Press.

Emerson, R. W. (any edition) "Memory" and "On education." In *Essays*.

Erasmus, D. (1992). "On education for children." In *Collected works of Erasmus*. Toronto and London: University of Toronto Press.

Gowers, Sir Ernest (1986). *The complete plain words* (3rd ed.), revised by S. Greenbaum & J. Whitcut. London: Penguin, 1986.

*Highet, G. (1989). *The art of teaching*. New York, NY: Vintage. This indispensible classic text on teaching was first published in 1950.

*James, W. (n.d.) *Talks to teachers on psychology and to students on some of life's ideals* (Mineoloa, NY: Dover Publications). One should also study *The principles of psychology* and read his various relevant essays, handily available in two volumes published by The Library of America.

Kant, I. (2003). *On education*, trans. A. Churton. Mineola, NY: Dover Publications. Also worth reading is his famous essay, "What is Enlightenment?"

*Laski, H. (1930). "The academic mind" and "teacher and student." In *The dangers of obedience and other essays*. New York, NY: Harper & Bros.

*Locke, J. (1996). *Some Thoughts Concerning Education* and *of the Conduct of the Understanding*, eds. Ruth W. Grant and Nathan Tarcov (Indianapolis, IN: Hackett Publishing Co., 1996). More ambitious readers will undertake his *Essay Concerning Human Understanding*.

*Lynch, J. (2008). *The English Language: A User's Guide*. Newburyport, MA: Focus Publishing.

Suggested Readings 131

This book is available online: http://andromeda.rutgers.edu/~jlynch/Writing/.
Marrou, H. I. (1964). *A history of education in antiquity*, trans. G. Lamb. New York. Also worth consulting is K. J. Freeman (1969). *Schools of Hellas*. New York, NY: Teacher's College Press.
Milton, J. (1951). *Areopagitica and of education*, Ed. G. Sabine. Croft's Classics.
Mill J. S. (1957). *The autobiography*. New York, NY: Bobbs-Merrill., chapters 1–3. Also read *On liberty*, chapter. 5 and the "Inaugural address delivered to the University of St. Andrews" (1867) in *Essays on equality, law, and education* (Toronto, 1984). This book is available online at the Online Library of Liberty of the Liberty Fund.
*Montaigne, M. (1976). *The complete essays*, trans. D. Frame. Stanford: Stanford University Press.
Essays: "Of pedantry"; "Of the education of children"; "Of the art of discussion"; "Of the vanity of words"; "Of books."
Newman J. H. (1986). *The idea of a university*. Notre dame: University of Notre Dame Press.
Null, J. W. & Ravitch D. (Eds.). *Forgotten Heroes of American Education: The Great Tradition of Teaching Teachers*. Greenwich, CT: Information Age Publishing.
*Orwell, G. (1950). "Politics and the English language" (1946). In *Shooting an elephant and other essays*. New York: Harcourt, Brace [1950].
This essay can be found online at various sites.
Peterson, H. (Ed.). (n.d.). *Great teachers, portrayed by those who studied under them*. New York, NY: Vintage Books.
Pinker, S. (2009). *How the mind works*. New York, NY: W. W. Norton, 1997.
Plato (1997). *Complete works*, Ed., J. M. Cooper. Indianapolis, IN: Hackett Publishing. See especially *The Republic*, *The Laws*, *Gorgias*, and *Phaedrus*.
*Plutarch (1960). "On Listening to Lectures," In *Moralia* I, trans. F. C. Babbit. Cambridge, MA: Loeb Classical Library.
This essay (and translation) can be found online. While at it, read "The Education of Children."
Postamn, N. & Weingarthner, C. (1969). *Teaching as a subversive activity*. New York, NY: Delacorte Press.
Quintilian (1933). *Institutio oratoria*, trans. H. E. Butler. Cambridge, MA: Loeb Classical Library.
Rabelais, F. (1991). *The complete works*, trans. D. Frame. Berkeley, CA: University of California Press.
Rousseau (1979). *Emile, or On Education*, trans. A. Bloom. New York, NY: Basic Books.
Schopenhauer, A. (n.d.). *Essays*, trans. T. B. Saunders (A. L. Burt Co., n.d.). Of special interest are: "On books and reading"; "On authorship"; "On style"; "On men of learning;" "On thinking for Oneself."
*Strunk, W. (2002). The elements of style. Mineola, NY: Dover Publications.
This book was first published in 1919.
*Thoreau, H. D. (1947) *Walden*. In Carl Bode (Ed.), *The portable Thoreau*., New York, NY: Penguin Books.
See especially the chapter on Reading
Van Doren M. (1943). *Liberal education*. New York, NY: Henry Holt.

Vives, J. L. (1913). *On education*, trans. F. Watson. Cambridge: Cambridge University Press.

Also see *The education of a christian woman: A sixteenth-century manual*, trans. C. Fantazzi. Chicago, IL: University of Chicago Press, 2000.

Whitehead, A. N. (1961). *The aims of education*. New York, NY: Mentor Books.

Zinsser, W. K.(2001). *On Writing Well, 25th Anniversary: The classic guide to writing nonfiction*. New York, NY: Collins.

ACKNOWLEDGMENTS

I would like to thank Mark Bauerlein, William Pannapacker, Sandra Stotsky, and Joe Simplicio for reviewing the manuscript and making invaluable suggestions on how to improve it. I would also like to thank my good friend Scott Irelan both for his support for this project from beginning to end and for serving as a sounding board for the material in this book. In addition, I wish to thank John Leo at *Minding the Campus* for giving me a venue to air some of my views, and for allowing me to use some of the material from my essays here. I wish to thank the editors at *Teaching History: A Journal of Methods*, in particular, Stephen Kneeshaw, for giving me permission to reprint the article I published in that journal. (A shorter version of Chapter 3 appeared in the Fall 2011 edition.) And I wish to thank George Johnson at Information Age Publishing for publishing this book. Finally, I would like to thank my wife Sarah Nies for her constant encouragement and support for every project that I have undertaken.

ABOUT THE AUTHOR

J. M. Anderson received his PhD in history from Syracuse University. He is the author of *The Honorable Burden of Public Office: English Humanists and Tudor Politics in the Sixteenth Century*, and is currently working on a history of love from the twelfth to the twentieth centuries. He is dean of Humanities, Fine Arts, and Social Sciences at Illinois Valley Community College.